PICTA DICTA
LATIN PRIMER
Volume 1

Teacher Guide

LATIN PRIMER

Volume 1
Teacher Guide

Reuben Jansen and Tim Griffith
Illustrations by Reuben Jansen

PICTA DICTA

Picta Dicta LLC | Moscow, Idaho

© 2020 Picta Dicta LLC

Published by Picta Dicta LLC
811 Harold St.
Moscow, ID 83843 | www.pictadicta.com

Picta Dicta Latin Primer (vol. 1): Teacher Guide
Tim Griffith and Reuben Jansen
Illustrations by Reuben Jansen
Cover and interior design by Abbie Adkerson

Illustrations copyright © 2019 Reuben Jansen

Printed in the United States of America
ISBN 978-1-953012-01-2

All rights reserved. No part of this publication may be reproduced, stored in a retrieval system, or transmitted in any form by any means, electronic, mechanical, photocopy, recording, or otherwise, without prior permission of the author, except as provided by USA copyright law.

Table of Contents

Introduction 1

Instructions 3

    Projector Delivery 3

    Projector Setup 7

    App Login and Setup 8

    Using the Workbook 9

    Using the Quizzes 10

    Pacing and Schedule 10

    Pronunciation and Macrons 16

Lessons 19

2nd Declension Masculine Nouns ("us" words)

    Lesson 1: Plural and Ablative Case (after *in*) 19

    Lesson 2: Prepositions *Cum* and *Ab* 22

    Lesson 3: Ablative (after *Sub* and *Ex*) 24

    Lesson 4: Verbs 26

    Lesson 5: Accusative Case (after *ad* and *ante*) 27

    Lesson 6: Accusative (after *post, super,* and *apud*) 29

    Lesson 7: Direct Objects 31

    Lesson 8: Dative Case (Indirect Objects) 33

    Lesson 9: Genitive Case 35

    Lesson 10: Nominative Case 37

    Lesson 11: -ER words 40

2nd Declension Neuter Nouns ("um" words)

    Lesson 12: Nominative and Ablative (after *in, cum, ab, sub,* and *ex*) 41

    Lesson 13: Accusative (after *ad, ante, post, super,* and *apud*) 43

Lesson 14: Accusative (direct objects) 45

Lesson 15: Dative (indirect objects) 46

Lesson 16: Genitive 48

Lesson 17: Nominative Plural 50

1st Declension Feminine Nouns ("a" words)

Lesson 18: Nominative and Ablative (after *in, cum, ab, sub, ex,* and *de* 52

Lesson 19: Accusative (after *ad, ante, post, super, apud,* and *per*) 54

Lesson 20: Accusative (direct objects) 57

Lesson 21: Dative (indirect objects) 58

Lesson 22: Genitive 60

Lesson 23: Review 63

1st and 2nd declension plural endings

Lesson 24: Ablative Plural (after *in, cum, ab, sub, ex,* and *de*) 67

Lesson 25: Accusative Plural (after *ad, ante, post, super, apud,* and *per*) 72

Lesson 26: Accusative Plural 78

Lesson 27: Dative Plural (indirect objects) 79

Lesson 28: Genitive Plural 84

Lesson 29: Plural Verbs 89

Lesson 30: Review 92

Workbook Answer Key 93

Quiz Answer Key 104

Vocabulary Index 121

Classroom Lessons, Discussions, and Activities 127

Introduction

Overview

Picta Dicta Latin Primer is a first introduction to reading Latin suitable for either elementary or secondary students. It is a multimedia course, not only with readings and workbook exercises—but videos and app-based exercises as well. Students learn through all four language pathways (reading, writing, speaking, and hearing), which makes it both more enjoyable for them to learn and easier to retain.

Method

The approach to teaching is hybrid, incorporating elements from both the reading method (which emphasizes examples) and the grammatical method (which emphasizes rules). Students begin each lesson by memorizing Latin words, phrases, or sentences for illustrated examples. These examples are carefully chosen to demonstrate the grammatical concept taught in the lesson.

After mastering examples, students watch a short video that explains the grammatical rule being taught. Students then revisit the examples they have memorized and analyze the forms used in each. This course does introduce grammatical terminology, but slowly—students learn one concept at a time and practice it to mastery.

At the end of each lesson, students watch an illustrated story using vocabulary and grammar they learned in the lesson. Students are delighted to discover that they can listen to and watch a story presented in an ancient language and understand it. After the story, students retell it or answer questions about it.

Scope

Picta Dicta Latin Primer is divided into two volumes. Elementary students typically complete one volume over the course of two years; jr. high students, over the course of one year; high school students may be able to complete both volumes in a single year. In the first volume, students learn about 200 Latin words, the basic uses of the five major noun cases, the noun endings of the 1st and 2nd declensions, and 3rd-person verbs of all four conjugations. In the second volume, students learn an additional 200 words, the 3rd, 4th, and 5th declensions, additional uses of the cases, adjective matching, and passive forms of verbs.

In-class lessons in the Teacher Guide and worksheets make it easy for teachers to introduce all three persons of the present indicative as well as imperative verbs through classroom chants and drills. These exercises lead teacher and students into basic conversational Latin around the classroom.

How is this course different?

Elementary Latin curricula often leave students burned-out after a year or two. This course is different. We love Latin, and it shows. We have designed every aspect of our curriculum to engage students deeply and get them to love Latin like we do. It is true that we have chosen material that is lighthearted and palatable for students; however, with every choice we made, we had helping your students towards excellence in mind.

We want to help your students love and understand language—not just Latin, but English and whatever other language they encounter later in life. We want to help them become doctors, lawyers, and engineers, who know how to pay close attention to details and understand complicated systems. We want to help them understand the modern world better by learning where it came from, how different the ancient world was, and how ancient people thought and spoke. We want to help them in their first steps toward reading some of the greatest literature ever written (Vergil's *Aeneid*, Ovid's *Metamorphoses*, Augustine's *Confessions*, Apuleius' *Cupid and Psyche*, etc.). In short, we want to help them have the kind of education that will help them be and do whatever they are meant to be and do.

Here are a few specific ways that we do it:

1. Picta Dicta's unique web platform gives students more practice and feedback than is possible in a print-only textbook. Over the course of each volume, a student sees almost 1,000 illustrated examples; he or she hears thousands of Latin words, phrases, and examples pronounced correctly every time; he or she receives immediate feedback for all answers given and has the opportunity to make corrections. This immediate feedback-correction loop builds skills quickly and reliably.

2. This course introduces students to the forms and concepts that are most practical for reading Latin, allowing them to begin understanding simple Latin stories after even the first lesson. Students using this curriculum do not wonder what the forms they are learning are used for. Every form is always connected to its function—they see each one used in concrete and intelligible ways over and over again.

3. Students using this course spend most of their time speaking or writing actual Latin—not English. This helps them learn it much more deeply, and (not insignificantly) gives them the thrill of speaking and writing in a different (and ancient) language. Why would anyone want to spend so much time and effort learning a language and still be unable to use it? In this course, your child will learn to use Latin as a language and will love it.

Instructions

Picta Dicta Latin Primer has five components for the classroom: the *Teacher Guide*, the *Student Workbook*, the *Quiz Pack*, Printable Worksheet PDFs, and a subscription to the *Picta Dicta Latin Primer* Application. Most schools will opt to receive the free PDF version of the Quiz Pack rather than purchase printed packets—which are necessarily pricy and take up a lot of space.

Instruction and exercises for this course are delivered in two ways: using a projector in front of a classroom, or through personal electronic devices such as laptops, desktops, or tablets. For schools that do not require or permit students to use technology, see instructions for Projector Delivery. For schools that do allow students to use personal devices, there are a couple options for Device Delivery.

Projector Delivery

Connect an internet-capable device to a large display with an audio system (SEE PROJECTOR SETUP BELOW) and access the Picta Dicta web platform (SEE APP LOGIN AND SETUP).

Navigate to the Play Dashboard and using the "Classroom" campaign of *Picta Dicta Latin Primer*, select the PLAY button to display lessons, exercises, and stories in front of a class. Select TRAIN to do optional exercises for each lesson.

Here are specific instructions and recommendations for each kind of projector-based activity:

Learn Vocab:

Learn Vocab is the first exercise for each lesson. In this exercise, students learn a few new nouns or verbs through pictures. The exercise proceeds in two steps: an introduction to new words and a multiple-choice exercise.

When teachers are first introducing words, the app will display a picture for the word; however, it will not pronounce the word unless the teacher clicks "pronunciation". This gives the teacher the opportunity to be the teacher and introduce the word herself.

Have students pronounce the Latin word in unison a couple times. Then single out a couple students to pronounce the word clearly. If the teacher is uncomfortable with Latin pronunciation, he can click or tap on the word on his device to replay the pronunciation. The app pronounces each word with special care to the length of each syllable, giving each word a unique rhythm and cadence. We recommend that teachers ensure that they follow this pronunciation carefully.

Discuss what the word means. Pictures are powerful for communicating meaning, but they can be misunderstood. Ask the class for two or three English words for what the picture is communicating. Latin words do not *mean* particular English words, so it is very helpful to discuss several possible English translations. For example, *puer* can be translated as "boy", but it is important for them to know that "kid", "lad", and "child" are good translations too. Whenever you teach a new word, ask the class for possible synonyms. This is a great opportunity to build their English vocabulary as well!

Have the students record each new vocabulary word, in the *Vocabula* section of their *Picta Dicta Latin Primer (vol. 1)* Workbook. They should record several English translations for each word where possible.

When the app switches to a multiple-choice exercise, notice that each choice has a letter by it. Have students write the correct letter on their whiteboard and hold them up for you. This is a soft-grading exercise: a teacher can see which students are understanding and which ones are not without having to record formal evaluations. At this point in the learning process, there is no reason to keep track of individual performance. Another way to do this is to have every student shout out the correct letter choice all at once—use a drop of the hand to get them all to answer at once. If a student gets a wrong answer, a teacher can usually hear it among the other correct ones.

Practice Vocab:

Practice Vocab is a reinforcement exercise for the new vocabulary. Instead of choosing words, the app will display a picture and the whole class should chant out the proper Latin word. It is important to ensure that students answer in unison. Again, use the drop of the hand or some other signal to get the class to answer all at once.

If time permits, run the Practice Vocab exercise again and have the students write out the answers on their white boards. Only give them a short time to give their answer. If they hold up the answer on their white board spelled correctly in time, have them give themselves a tally mark in one corner of their board. At the end of the exercise, give praise or a reward to the one with the most tally marks. In general, it is not a good idea to use these soft-grading exercises to give formal grades—this is a time for learning and practice.

Review Vocab:

Review Vocab is exactly like Practice Vocab except that it covers old words from previous chapters. If time is short, do this orally. If time permits, turn it into a spelling game on whiteboards.

Sentences:

In this exercise, the app will introduce new example sentences for the students to commit to memory. Just like with the vocabulary, have the students repeat the sentence with the same pronunciation and cadence as the voice on the app. If necessary, click or tap the sentence to hear it multiple times.

Often times, prepositions will be introduced in these sentences for the first time. This is a great time to ask the class if anyone can figure out what one of these means. The first time that the class sees the word *cum*, ask the students what *cum* is doing in the sentence. When they figure it out, have them all write it down in the *Vocabula* section of their Student Workbook.

It may be tempting to introduce a grammatical concept at this point, and students may begin to ask *why* an ending has changed or a particular word has been used. It is great when students figure out the rules on their own, but it is usually better to wait a little longer before discussing these. We recommend that you wait at least until the students have completed Exercise 1b before getting to the formal rules—more students will be able to be part of the discussion if you wait until they are a little more familiar with the sentences. Otherwise, you will be having a discussion with the quickest two students as the others are still trying to figure out what is going on.

Again, when the app proceeds to multiple-choice questions, have the students either shout out the correct letter choice or write it on white boards.

Exercise 1a:

This is more practice with multiple-choice questions; however, they will see and hear some sentences that they did not learn. This forces them to do some low-level pattern recognition. Have them shout out the entire answers or write them on their white boards. When you have been having students answer in unison for a bit, switch it up and call on someone randomly. Or, have the students all stand up and raise their hands to give an answer individually. When a student has been called on and has answered properly, ask them to sit down: *Conside!* (kohn-SEE-deh).

Exercise 1b:

In this exercise, students will see the whole sentence except for the ending. If you are pressed for time, you can have students shout out the answers. If you do this, it is recommended that you read out the entire sentence and have the students chime in when they get to the word with the missing ending. If you have a bit more time, you can have students write the endings out on their board. If you have enough time, you can ask them to write out the complete sentence with the proper ending. If someone makes a mistake, indicate that they made a mistake and give them an opportunity to correct it.

Lesson:

In this exercise, there is a short grammar lesson based on the examples the students have just learned. This lesson is presented by video in its entirety. A teacher has the option of displaying the video for the students or recreating the lesson themselves. The video lessons are short and efficient, but sometimes the students might enjoy watching the teacher draw the pictures on the board and teach the same lesson. There is something about horribly drawn stick figures that students find very gratifying, especially when they think they could do a better job themselves.

If a teacher wants to let the students figure out what the new pattern is and argue about why, this is a great time to do it. But to make sure the weaker students are following along, it is a good idea to play the video afterwards. The quicker students find it gratifying if they figured out the pattern and why before they learned it in the video.

At this point, students should record all new grammar terms and new rules in the *Regulae* ("rules") section of their Student Workbook.

Additionally, when a lesson introduces a new ending, students should write the ending in the appropriate chart in the *Tabulae* ("charts") section of their Student Workbook. You will notice that the charts in *Tabulae* are completely blank—not even the case names are filled in. The reason for this is to allow you, the teacher, to choose what order you wish to teach these cases. The American order is Nominative, Genitive, Dative, Accusative, and Ablative. The British order is

Nominative, Accusative, Genitive, Dative, and Ablative. This is particularly import if you wish to teach your students to chant the endings.

Occasionally, you will encounter a Lesson B if there is a second grammar lesson in the chapter. Follow the same techniques for introducing this material.

Exercise 2a:

This is another set of exercises like those in Exercise 1a. This time, take the opportunity to orally quiz the students on the grammar they have just learned. Ask them what case things are, whether a word is singular or plural, why an ending is *-o* instead of *-us,* etc.

Exercise 2b:

This exercise is designed for the students to write out the complete sentence. This is the hardest exercise because there are so many opportunities to make mistakes. You can begin by having them do these orally in unison. Then when they have gotten through them once, redo the exercise on white boards. This will take some time, but it is a great time to find any problems that need to be fixed before they do their first exercise in their workbook. When you see a mistake, give a hint and allow the student to fix it. For example, *I'm not so sure about the ending on that last word there,* or *Is that word supposed to be plural?*

Endings:

This is a fairly straightforward exercise that gives a sentence and asks a grammatical question about a word in that sentence. Teachers familiar with Latin will immediately notice that the app does not introduce *all* the technical terminology up front. For example, words in the nominative case are called "normal" for several lessons into the course. The program will eventually use the proper technical terms, but very slowly. If you think it better to teach additional terminology, feel free to do so. But in general, the younger students are, the more trouble they have accumulating technical concepts. *Picta Dicta Latin Primer* tries to minimize how many are introduced at one time and gives students plenty of time to internalize their meaning.

You can have students write the proper letter on their board, but it is better and faster to have the students all give the correct answer in unison (at the drop of a hand). This makes it go quicker. Every once in a while, stop after a question and ask a random student why it was the right answer.

A good way to step up the difficulty of this exercise is to have students write out the entire sentence and label everything they know about in it. This becomes particularly useful toward the end of the course when they know a fair bit of terminology for the things going on in any given sentence.

Verbs is a variation on this exercise that focuses on verb endings instead of noun endings. Use the same techniques in class.

Story:

Story is a video-based narration of a Latin story using the words and grammar they have learned. There are often a couple interjections or conjunctions introduced in a story. You can have them watch the story first (maybe twice), and then discuss what the extra words mean. Someone in the class will probably be able to guess from context. This is always the best—inferring from context is an essential skill in reading difficult Latin later on.

Once you have discussed them as a class, have students write any new conjunctions or interjections in the *Vocabula* ("Vocabulary Words") section of their Student Workbook.

At the end of some stories, students will answer a comprehension question about the story they have just seen and heard. Have the students answer in unison.

Retell:

In Retell, students are required to remember what happens next in a story. They will see a picture and hear the Latin. When the teacher advances to the multiple-choice screen, they will have to choose which sentence comes next. If you are short on time, give them a moment to think and then have them say it aloud in unison. If you have more time, you can have them write the letter or even the entire sentence out.

Projector Setup

To use a projector or other large screen in a classroom setting, you will need to access the Picta Dicta web app at app.pictadicta.com on another device first. We recommend the following devices:

- ♦ a PC or Mac computer using an updated Chrome or Firefox browser
- ♦ an iOS device (iPhone or iPad) with the Picta Dicta web address (app.pictadicta.com) added to homescreen
- ♦ an Android device using the Picta Dicta app from the app store
- ♦ a Kindle Fire using the Picta Dicta app from the Amazon app store

Access the Picta Dicta web platform on your device (SEE APP LOGIN AND SETUP) and navigate to the "Play Dashboard". An instructor should already be enrolled in a "Teacher" campaign. This campaign is customized for teachers who display lessons and exercises in front of a classroom.

If you display your screen from a PC or Mac, you can use a wireless remote (such as is used for navigating through PowerPoint slides) to advance through the exercises. It is particularly useful if you have a remote with a built-in laser pointer. This allows you to point at particular items on the screen while walking around the classroom.

If you display your screen from a phone, we recommend that you lock your screen in horizontal orientation. This will take the most advantage of your screen space.

App Login and Setup

To use the Picta Dicta web platform:

Setup:

1. On a PC or Mac, use the Chrome or Firefox browser to go to app.pictadicta.com
2. Register a new account unless you have already been set up with one.
3. If you have not already been supplied with a subscription, you may need to obtain a subscription code. Contact info@pictadicta.com to make a school order. Go to Subscriptions and paste your subscription code to get access to your course.
4. Under Learner Profiles, create profiles for any learners who will be using the app.
5. Click on the enroll button by each learner and select *Latin Primer*.
6. Choose a campaign (difficulty level). We recommend Classroom for most classrooms.

Play:

1. Log in with the username and password you gave to the learner or click on the learner's username from the Account page.
2. When your account loads up, you will see the *Picta Dicta Latin Primer*.
3. Click on PLAY to start the first exercise.

To use the Picta Dicta web application on individual devices:

1. Select a device that works for the age of the students. Picta Dicta's web application works very well on a PC or Mac, tablet, or smart phone. We recommend that you use either the Chrome or Firefox web browser for the best performance. Safari works as well, but Internet Explorer is not supported.

   For younger students, a touch tablet works best. Kindle Fire works particularly well. If using a Kindle device, download the Picta Dicta app from the Amazon app store. If using an iOS tablet, make sure to add the Picta Dicta web app to your homescreen:

   ♦ Go to https://app.pictadicta.com in your Safari web browser (on your iOS device)

   ♦ Click on the share button and select add to home screen

   ♦ The Picta Dicta app should now appear on your iOS home screen as an app

2. Your student should be able to hear the audio clearly. If there is a lot of ambient noise, headphones are recommended. Background music is not recommended unless the volume is low.

3. Your student should repeat the Latin words and phrases trying to match the pronuncia-

tion as closely as possible. Some students will do this naturally; others will need to be encouraged to repeat the words aloud. This is essential for committing the material to memory.

4. As your student begins to master a lesson, he or she should try to say the correct answers aloud before advancing to multiple choice screens. This pushes a student to memorize the details actively—not merely recognize them.

5. Keep vocab notes. There is a section called *Vocabula* ("words") toward the end of the workbook. Whenever your student learns a new word, he or she should write it in that section for review later—the word and a word or two to translate (e.g., *puer* - boy, kid).

6. Keep grammar notes. There is a section called *Regulae* ("rules") toward the end of the workbook. Whenever your student watches a grammar lesson, he or she should copy down new grammar terms and rules in this section for review later (e.g., *The ablative case comes after the word "in"*).

7. Keep chart notes. There is a section called Tabulae ("charts") toward the end of the workbook. Whenever your student learns a new form in a grammar lesson, he or she should write that ending down in the appropriate chart. Each lesson will tell where a student is supposed to write this information.

8. At the end of an exercise, the app will sometimes give a score in stars. Five stars is perfect; one star means it took a while to get them all correct. A student should generally try to get at least three or four stars before moving on. It is always possible to replay an exercise to get a better score.

Using the Workbook

♦ A student should use a pencil when writing Latin. Mistakes are common in Latin, so he or she should be ready to erase answers.

♦ It is easier to have your student write in print rather than cursive. Reading (and correcting) Latin is hard enough without trying to see subtle letters in cursive like "i".

♦ When your student has finished filling out a page, check the answers against the answer key on page 93 of this Teacher Guide. Circle any wrong words or endings in pencil; then allow your student to attempt to correct them without hearing or seeing the correct answer. Mistakes and misspelling are normal and common in Latin. Correction is an important step in the learning process.

♦ Encourage your student to write neatly. In many years of teaching Latin, I have observed that those who write neatly consistently make fewer mistakes!

♦ Check the vocabulary, grammar, and chart notes that your student takes in the back of the workbook with the answer key on page 121 of this guide. If a student makes a mistake, have him or her correct it. (The order of the vocabulary and grammar notes is not particularly important.)

Using the Quizzes

- ♦ We generally recommend that schools use the free PDF of the quiz pack instead of purchasing individual colored quiz packs. There are not only more quizzes available in this version, but the cost of color quizzes is often prohibitive for schools.

- ♦ A student should use a pencil, so he or she can fix any mistakes.

- ♦ A key for the Quiz Pack is provided at the end of this guide on page 104.

- ♦ When grading a quiz, it is a good idea to circle any wrong answers and allow corrections. Give *at least* half credit for a corrected answer—depending on the age of the student. For example, if a student gets 1 out of 10 questions wrong at first—but corrects it, he or she should receive a score of *at least* 9.5/10. For younger students, it may be wise not to penalize corrections at all.

- ♦ If a student consistently does poorly on quizzes, check to see how many stars he or she is receiving on the Picta Dicta Latin Primer app. If the student is getting lower scores (one or two stars), have the student start redoing the games to improve scores. It is better to go a little slower than to miss the concepts. If a student does well on the app but poorly on written assignments, allow him or her to consult vocabulary, grammar, and chart notes from the workbook.

Pacing and Schedule

Picta Dicta Latin Primer (vol. 1) has 30 lessons, each of which lesson can be covered in one week or two—depending on your goals. Time required each day will depend heavily on the student (10 - 30 minutes). Keep in mind that some app-based exercises only appear in some lessons—these are enclosed in parentheses. Some lessons will take more time than others, so there is nothing wrong (or unusual) about getting a bit behind schedule. If students get behind schedule, it is much better to take an extra week to catch up than to rush through material. The app-based exercises for Volume 1 are also included in a subscription for Volume 2! So, your students can always complete the last chapters of Volume 1 in the next year without any problem—if it is needed.

App-based Exercises

For app-based exercises, your child should use the username and password that you set up for him to access his own learn profile (see setup instructions above). Your students should just have to select PLAY to proceed to the next exercise. He can replay any exercise by clicking on the "redo" button by the star score for the exercise.

Student Workbook

A student does four different exercises in his *Student Workbook*. First, he records all new vocabulary words in the *Vocabula* (voh-KAH-boo-lah) section beginning on page 63. Second, he records all new grammar rules and terms in the *Regulae* (RAY-ghoo-laye) section beginning on page 78. Third, he records all new endings in the *Tabulae* (TAH-boo-laye) section beginning on page 85—there are charts for him to copy in the lesson guides for each chapter where endings are introduced. Fourth, he does *Lessons a* and *b* for each lesson.

✓ Evaluation

Teachers should generally go over written work as a class and allow students to make corrections. From time to time, it is a good idea to spot check each students' individual work—whether for a grade or not.

💬 Discussion

Ideally, a teacher should regularly dialogue with the students on the material. First, it is important to actually discuss new vocabulary to ensure that they understand the words. Second, it is important to discuss the new grammar lessons with the students to ensure that the new endings and rules make sense to them. Third, a teacher should do the *Check-in* questions with the students at the end of each lesson to see if they are ready to go on. The lessons guides for each guide give all the information necessary to have these discussions.

✔ Quiz

The students should take two quizzes from the *Quiz Pack* (PDF or print) for each lesson: the *Vocabula* Quiz over vocabulary early in the week, and or *Sententiae* Quiz at the end of the week. The PDF Quiz Pack can be printed in black and white, but displayed in full color on a projector to save on printing costs.

One-Week Schedule

Monday:

- 🎮 *Learn Vocab*
- 🎮 *Practice Vocab*
- 🎮 *(Review Vocab)*
- ✏️ *Vocabula*
- ✅ *Vocabula*
- 💬 *Vocabula*
- 🗒️ *Vocabula* Quiz
- ✅ *Vocabula* Quiz

Tuesday:

- 🎮 *Sentences*
- 🎮 *Exercise 1a*
- 🎮 *Exercise 1b*
- 🎮 *Lesson*
- ✏️ *Regulae*
- 🎮 *(Endings)*
- ✅ *Regulae*

Wednesday:

- ✏️ *Lesson a (e.g., Lesson 1a)*
- ✅ *Lesson a*
- 💬 Lesson
- ✏️ *Tabulae*
- 🎮 Exercise 2a
- 🎮 Exercise 2b

Thursday:

🎮 *(Grammar Review)*

🎮 *(Lesson B)*

🎮 *(Endings)*

💬 *(Lesson B)*

✏️ *Lesson b (e.g., Lesson 1b)*

✅ *Lesson b*

Friday:

🎮 Story/ Story+

🎮 Retell/Story Questions

📋 *Sententiae* Quiz

✅ *Sententiae* Quiz

💬 *Parental Check-in*

💬 *Lesson Checklist*

Two-Week Schedule

Monday:

🎮 *Learn Vocab*

🎮 *Practice Vocab*

🎮 *(Review Vocab)*

✏️ *Vocabula*

✅ *Vocabula*

💬 *Vocabula*

Tuesday:

📋 *Vocabula* Quiz

✅ *Vocabula* Quiz

Wednesday:

🎮 *Sentences*

🎮 *Exercise 1a*

🎮 *Exercise 1b*

Thursday:

🎮 *Lesson*

✏️ *Regulae*

🎮 *(Endings)*

✅ *Regulae*

Friday:

✏️ *Lesson a (e.g., Lesson 1a)*

✅ *Lesson a*

💬 Lesson

✏️ *Tabulae*

Monday:

- 🎮 *Exercise 2a*
- 🎮 Exercise 2b

Tuesday:

- 🎮 *(Grammar Review)*
- 🎮 *(Lesson B)*
- 🎮 *(Endings)*
- 💬 (Lesson B)
- ✏️ *Lesson b (e.g., Lesson 1b)*
- ✅ *Lesson b*

Wednesday:

- 🎮 Story/Story+
- 🎮 Retell/Story Questions

Thursday:

- 📋 *Sententiae Quiz*
- ✅ *Sententiae Quiz*

Friday:

- 💬 *Parental Check-in*
- 💬 *Lesson Checklist*

Pronunciation and Macrons

This course uses a classical pronunciation of Latin. This is an approximation of how the Romans spoke the language as opposed to how people spoke Latin during the Middle Ages (Ecclesiastical Latin). Even though Latin uses the same alphabet as English, the letters and letter combinations are often pronounced differently. The app-based exercises in this course make it easy for children to pronounce every word correctly because they hear it and repeat it. We also have provided pronunciation for all of the vocabulary lists throughout this guide. That said, it may still be necessary to go over Latin phonics with your child to help him with spelling.

Note that there is some variation even within classical pronunciation. In particular, some teachers like to pronounce the v as a very strong "w". Historically, some Romans pronounced this letter as a soft "w"; others pronounced it as something between a "w" and a "v" called a bilabial fricative. Any pronunciation from a "w" to a "v" is acceptable. The app pronunciation will sound more like a "v". If you prefer the "w" sound, feel free to teach it to your child.

If you are experienced with Latin, you may wonder whether this course uses macrons to show vowel lengths. As a rule, this course does not print macrons unless they are critical for understanding a form. We have chosen to omit them because it is much easier for young children to hear the vowel lengths rather than see and write them. Every word in this course is pronounced according to its proper vowel lengths, so students do not need macrons in order to determine the proper pronunciation. That said, if you wish to have your students learn macrons, write us at info@pictadicta.com, and we will provide you with a PDF supplement of the complete vocabulary for this course with macrons

Pronunciation Guide

a	AH (as in "father")
b	B (as in "bike")
c	K (as in "cat")
d	D (as in "dog")
e	EH (as in "let") or AY (as in "day")
f	F (as in "fight")
g	GH (as in "get")
h	H (as in "hot")
i	(vowel) – I (as in "pin") or EE (as in "free")
i	(consonant) – Y (as in "yell")
l	L (as in "light")
m	M (as in "mop")
n	N (as in "napkin")
o	OH (as in "boat")
p	P (as in "paper")
qu	KW (as in "quick")
r	R (rolled or trilled like "burrito" would be in Spanish)
s	S (as in "gas")—never a "z" sound
t	T (as in "tack")
u	OO (as in "push")
v	V (as in "valley") or W (as in "wind")
x	KS (as in "axe")
z	Z (as in "zone")
ae	AYE (as in "pie")
au	OW (as in "cow")
eu	EW (as in "few")
ch	KH ("*kh*aki")

Lesson 1

Vocabula

Whenever students learn new vocabulary words, have them copy the words and some English translations down in the Vocabula ("Vocabulary Words") section of their student workbook on page 63. Come up with several English equivalents as a class as they write them down. This turns it into a class discussion and makes them think about the meaning more. It is usually better to have students learn and practice the words on the app exercises (in class or individually) first before writing them down. The extra notes for words do not need to be copied down, but are given so that teachers can answer any questions the students may have about the words. The students will learn most new words in the Learn Vocab exercise, but there will sometimes be some extras in the grammar exercises or story.

- *puer* - boy; this is also the general word for "kid" when you don't know the gender
- *oculus* - eye
- *stilus* - pen; a Roman stylus was used for writing on a wax tablet, but it works for "pen" for now
- *digitus* - finger; the Romans also used this word for "toe"
- *campus* - meadow; an open clearing, not a field where crops are grown
- *fluvius* - river; this could be used for a "flow" of anything or even a creek or stream.
- *hortus* - garden; this can be used of both vegetable and flower gardens

- *est* - is; there are lots of forms of this, but you will just use this one for a while
- *in* - in; sometimes this can be translated "on"

- *ubi?* - where?; this can also be used like the non-question "where" (*Puer est ubi fluvius est.*)
- *estne* - is it …?; adding *ne* to the end of a word makes a yes or no question
- *non* - not; this word can also be used for giving the answer, "no"
- *finis* - the end; we'll use this at the end of every story

Take special care that the students understand that *campus* refers to a "meadow", not "grass". Also, the Latin preposition *in* can be translated "in" but sometimes it can be translated "on". It may not be necessary to bring this up, but it may come up as a question during the exercises.

Lesson: Singular and Plural

For the first eight lessons, *Picta Dicta Latin Primer* focuses on 2nd-declension masculine nouns--for now we call these "-*us* words" (pronounced "oos") because we want to focus on concepts first before we start introducing a lot of technical terms. We do not even call them "nouns" yet until they learn about the difference between nouns and adjectives. If the student already knows the terms "declension", "noun", and "masculine", it would be a good idea to point out that the "-*us* words" are 2nd-declension masculine nouns. Otherwise, there is no need to explain it yet.

Keep in mind that this course has students memorize examples first, then rules. So when a student first learns new grammar, he or she will see it used first. Some students may immediately ask, "Why did the ending change?". If they do, turn the question back on them: "The rule is coming soon, but see if you can guess it first. Why do *you* think the ending changed?" When they get to the "Lesson" exercise with the grammar video, the rule will be explained very clearly, and they should write it down carefully in the *Regulae* section of their student workbook.

When an "-*us* word" is made plural, the ending changes to -*i*. So, there is one *oculus* (eye) but there are two *oculi* (eyes). You see this in some English words like one *octopus* and two *octopi*.

Regulae

Have your students copy down all new rules and definitions in the *Regulae* ("Rules") section of their student workbook on page 78. From time to time, it is a great idea to quiz your class on these rules to review them. Or, have students form into pairs and quiz each other on old rules.

- *singular* - a word that means only one
- *plural* - a word that means two or more
- A word that ends in -*us* usually changes to the ending -*i* in the plural.

Tabulae

Have your students copy down all new endings in the *Tabulae* ("Charts") section of their student workbook on page 85. Have them use a pencil to fill in the chart because later on they will need to add or change a few items.

Before you start having students fill out the charts in the back of their workbooks, you will need to decide which order of cases you want to use. The traditional order is nominative, genitive, dative, accusative, and ablative. However, the "British" order is nominative, accusative, genitive, dative, ablative. There are some advantages to using the British order later on, but consistency is the most important thing. If the students have learned to chant endings or the secondary-level teachers in your school use the traditional order, you should as well. We have deliberately allowed you as the teacher to choose which order. We will give both options (if they differ) whenever students need to copy down new endings.

Tabulae (Traditional & British Order)

CASE	FUNCTION	SG.	PL.
Normal		**US**	**I**

Lesson B: Ablative Case

When an -*us* word comes after the preposition *in*, the ending changes to -*o*. The word *fluvius* changes to *fluvio* in the sentence, *Puer in fluvio est.* ("The boy is in the river."). This ending is called the ablative case.

Regulae

- *case* - an ending that shows how a word works in a sentence
- *ablative* - the ending that is used after certain words, such as *in*.
- A word that ends in *-us* usually changes to *-o* in the ablative case.
- The word after *in* changes to the ablative case.

Tabulae (Traditional & British Order)

CASE	FUNCTION	SG.	PL.
Normal		US	I
Ablative	**After in**	**O**	

Lesson 2

Vocabula

- *ambulat* - walks; this is the first verb other than *est*, but they will learn about verbs later
- *servus* - servant; this word could also be translated as "slave"
- *dominus* - master; this word could also be translated as "owner"
- *lupus* - wolf; the wolf was the most common "bad character" in Roman fables
- *murus* - wall; this only refers to a wall around a city, not the side of a room
- *mundus* - world; this word often means the "whole universe", not just a "planet"
- *gladius* - sword

- ab - from, away form

- cum - with, together with
- *iam* - now

In this lesson there are three new vocabulary words, *dominus, servus,* and *murus,* which have faded portions in their illustrations. The new vocabulary word refers to the portion that is not faded. The faded portion is there because the word is difficult to depict on its own without context. For instance, a servant is understood as subjected to his master, and a fortifying wall is understood as protecting that which it encloses. Make sure that the students understand this when learning the new vocabulary. Also point out that a *murus* goes around a city, not around a room.

If you are very familiar with Latin, you know that the letter "b" frequently drops out of the Latin preposition "ab" before consonants. So a Roman author would probably write **a** *fluvio* instead of **ab** *fluvio*. This rule can be extremely confusing to younger students, so in this course we retain the "b" even before consonants. This compromise helps a student focus on the weightier rules of Latin for now; he or she can learn that the "b" drops out later in his or her education.

Lesson: Prepositions

In the last lesson you learned that "in" takes a word in the ablative case. A word like "in" that must have a word following it is called a preposition. *Cum* and *ab* are two more Latin prepositions that take a word in the ablative case. This word that comes after a preposition is called the "object of the preposition" in grammar. If students are already familiar with this term from English class, use it. If not, it is usually better to not introduce too many technical terms all at once.

Regulae

- *preposition* - a word that always goes with another word right behind it
- The word after the prepositions *in, cum,* and *ab* goes in the ablative case.

Tabulae (Traditional & British Order)

CASE	FUNCTION	SG.	PL.
Normal		US	I
Ablative	After *prepositions* in, *cum,* and *ab*	O	

Lesson 3

Vocabula

- *petasus* - hat; the word means a hat with a brim, not a cap
- *equus* - horse; this could also refer to a pony
- *cibus* - food
- *anulus* - ring; married Romans wore rings on their ring finger, like we do
- *calceus* - shoe; a Roman shoe was often more like a sandal

- *sub* - under
- *ex* - out of, off of

- *et* - and
- *sed* - but
- *nemo* - nobody; some words end in -o in their normal form--this is not the ablative case

Just as the letter *b* often drops out of the preposition *ab*, the *x* frequently drops out of *ex* in front of a word beginning with a consonant. However, we have again chosen not to observe this rule for the present time. Students can get very confused because they think *ex* and *e* are two different words.

Students may have a little trouble distinguishing between *ab* and *ex* since the difference between the two words is slight. *Ab* shows that something is moving *away from* something. *Ex* shows similar movement away but also that the something began inside of or on top of it. So *ex* can mean something like *out of, out from inside of, out from among, off of, off from the top of,* etc. It may seem easier just to give an English translation, but it is not. Show the student that *ex* means that the thing began *in*, but *ab* does not.

When students ask about it, try demonstrating the difference between *ab* and *ex* with props or the whiteboard in your classroom. Draw some flowers on one side of the whiteboard (enough that they can be seen on either side of you if you stand in front), point to them, and say, "hortus" to the class. Stand visibly *beside* them, and say, "Magister (or magistra) cum horto est." Have the students repeat. Then walk away from them. Say, "Magister ab horto ambulat." Have the students repeat. Then stand right in front of the flowers, so it looks like you are in among them. Say, "Magister in horto est." Have the student repeat. Now, walk "out of the garden" to the other side of the board and say, "Magister ex horto ambulat." Have the students repeat. After an exercise like this, it is good to have a discussion with the students about it. Ask them, "What happened there? When did we say *ab* and when did we say *ex*?"

Lesson: *Sub* & *Ex*

Lesson three introduces two more prepositions, *sub* and *ex*. These two prepositions also take the ablative case.

Regulae

- The prepositions *in, ab, cum, ex,* and *sub* take a word in the ablative case.

Tabulae (Traditional & British Order)

CASE	FUNCTION	SG.	PL.
Normal		US	I
Ablative	After prepositions in, cum, ab, *ex, and sub*	O	

Lesson 4

Vocabula

- *dormit* - sleeps
- *legit* - reads; Romans generally read aloud instead of silently
- *scribit* - writes
- *sedet* - sits
- *stat* - stands
- *cogitat* - thinks; this word means to "do some thinking", not to "have an opinion"

- *dum* - while

One of the examples for this lesson says, *Puer stat.* ("The boy stands.") For the purposes of this course, a person counts as "standing" only if a person is standing akimbo (with his hands on his hips and his elbows out). In other instances, someone may be standing, but the verb to use will be *est*. For example, if the boy is under a sword with his hands on his hips, understand it as, *Puer sub gladio stat.* But if the boy is under a sword and his hands are not on his hips, understand as, *Puer sub gladio est*. This, of course, does not have anything to do with the actual meaning--it is just a teaching device.

Lesson: Verbs

If you know much Latin, you will know that there are different classes of verbs based on the vowel that comes before the ending. These are called conjugations, and they can be a bit confusing. In this course, we use simplified descriptive terms. We call them a-verbs (1st conjugation), e-verbs (2nd conjugation), consonant-verbs (3rd conjugation), weak i-verbs (3rd (-io) conjugation), and strong i-verbs (4th conjugation). If none of that makes sense, do not worry! For now, students learn three things: 1) a-verbs have an "a" before the ending "-t", 2) e-verbs have an "e" before the ending "-t", and 3) other verbs have an "i" before the "t". We will distinguish between the other types of verbs later. For now, they should simply be able to recognize the difference between a-verbs, e-verbs, and other kinds of verbs.

Regulae

- *verb* - a word that usually shows an action
- A-verbs have an *a* before the ending -*t*.
- E-verbs have an e before the ending -*t*.
- Other kinds of verbs end in -*it*.

Lesson 5

Vocabula

- *capillus* - hair; this word only refers to hair on the head
- *nasus* - nose
- *ventus* - wind
- *filius* - son
- *circulus* - circle
- *cavus* - hole; this could refer to a hole in the ground or a hole in a tree, big or small

- *ante* - in front of; this can be used to refer to time to mean "before"
- *ad* - to; this word almost always shows movement "towards" something
- *quoque* - too; this word comes after the word being added, like "too" or "as well"

Lesson: Accusative Case

This lesson teaches two new prepositions, but this time the "-*us* word" after the preposition is going to change in a different way. After the prepositions *ad* and *ante* the -*us* ending changes to -*um*. This ending is called the accusative case. In Latin, some prepositions take the ablative case, and others take the accusative case. Most prepositions take the accusative case, but the most important prepositions (like *in* and *cum*) usually take the ablative case.

Help your students recognize that the five prepositions they already know (*in*, *cum*, *ab*, *sub*, and, *ex*) should be in a different category in their minds from the two they learn this week (*ad* and *ante*). Those first five take the ablative case (-*o*), and the two new prepositions take the accusative case (-*um*).

Regulae

- *accusative* - a new case used after some prepositions and in some other places
- The prepositions *ad* and *ante* take a word in the accusative case.

Tabulae (Traditional Order)

CASE	FUNCTION	SG.	PL.
Normal		US	I
Accusative	**After prepositions *ad* and *ante***	**UM**	
Ablative	After prepositions *in*, *cum*, *ab*, *ex*, and *sub*	O	

Tabulae (British order)

CASE	FUNCTION	SG.	PL.
Normal		US	I
Accusative	**After prepositions *ad* and *ante***	**UM**	
Ablative	After prepositions *in*, *cum*, *ab*, *ex*, and *sub*	O	

Lesson 6

Vocabula

- *nummus* - coin
- *saccus* - bag
- *ursus* - bear
- *asinus* - donkey
- *sacculus* - purse; a pouch for holding something small in
- *maritus* - husband; this word can also mean "groom"

- *super* - above; this word can mean "on top of" and "over"
- *post* - behind; this word can also be used of time to mean "after"
- *apud* - at; this word usually means "located at" and is usually used with places

- *quis?* - who?

In this lesson students learn the preposition *apud*, which has a similar meaning to the preposition *cum* they have learned before--but there is a difference. *Apud* is a better word to use with a place like a *fluvius* or *hortus*; *cum* is a better word to use with a person or an item (like a *gladius*). In English *apud* is often translated as "near" or "at", and *cum* is translated "with" or "together with".

By this point students have gotten to a point where they know enough Latin to describe a scene in more than one way. They know the words *super* ("above") and *sub* ("below"), as well as *ante* ("in front of") and *post* ("behind"). These sets of opposites allow us to describe scenes in more than one way. If the wolf is over (*super*) the garden, then the garden is also under (*sub*) the wolf. Both answers describe the same scene, but in order to avoid confusion, we recommend you teach the following rule: start with the person or animal--not with an inanimate object. For example, since a wolf is an animal and a garden is not, you should teach students to say and write, *Lupus super hortum est*, instead of *Hortus sub lupo est*. If there are two people or animals, you should teach them to go from left to right.

Even though this is how the "right" answers work in this course, you can use the fact that there are other possibilities as an exercise in class. Ask the students, "How else could we describe this scene? What if we started with *hortus*?" Also consider giving full- or nearly full-credit for giving an alternate answer on a workbook exercise or quiz.

Lesson: *Post, Super, & Apud*

In this lesson students learn three new prepositions: *post*, *super*, and *apud*. Like *ad* and *ante*, these prepositions take the accusative case.

Make sure students understand that there are two kinds of prepositions: prepositions that take the ablative case (*in, cum, ab, sub, ex*) and prepositions that take the accusative case (*ad, ante, post, super, apud*). It is very important not to confuse which are which, so it is good to review each list frequently. Consider having the students chant out the list in class.

Teacher: "Prepositions that take the ablative!"
Students: "*in, cum, ab, sub, ex*!"

Teacher: "Prepositions that take the accusative!"
Students: "*ad, ante, post, super, apud*!"

Ideally your students have memorized the sentence examples so well that they are able to remember which preposition takes which ending by memory. However, memory of the examples should be confirmed by reciting the rule. If students need to know which ending *cum* takes, some will remember the example, *Puer cum lupo est* and realize that it takes the "o" ending. However, others will remember the rule: *cum* takes the ablative case. Frequent review of rules and examples are the best way to ensure success for the whole class.

Regulae

- The prepositions *post*, *apud*, and *super* take a word in the accusative case.

Tabulae (Traditional Order)

CASE	FUNCTION	SG.	PL.
Normal		US	I
Accusative	After prepositions *ad, ante, **post, super,** and **apud***	UM	
Ablative	After prepositions *in, cum, ab, ex,* and *sub*	O	

Tabulae (British Order)

CASE	FUNCTION	SG.	PL.
Normal		US	I
Accusative	After prepositions *ad, ante, **post, super,** and **apud***	UM	
Ablative	After prepositions *in, cum, ab, ex,* and *sub*	O	

Lesson 7

Vocabula

- *amicus* - friend
- *pulsat* - hits; this could also be translated as "knock" if the object is a door
- *videt* - sees
- *habet* - has; this can mean "own" or "have on one's person"
- *agnus* - lamb
- *delphinus* - dolphin
- *immo* - instead; this is a word used to introduce a correction

Lesson: Direct Object

The direct object is the noun in the sentence that receives the action of the verb. "Wall" is the direct object in the following sentence: "The boy punches the wall".

In Latin, when a word is the direct object in a sentence, its ending changes to accusative. So an *-us* word like *murus* changes to the accusative (*murum*) when it is a direct object. Before now we have seen the accusative after certain prepositions, but its primary purpose is to show the direct object. So when an *-us* word is a direct object in Latin, its ending changes to *-um*. Since "wall" was the direct object in the sentence we saw a moment ago, in Latin, it becomes *puer mur**um** pulsat*.

In English you must be very careful with the order of your words in a sentence. "The boy punches the wall" and "the wall punches the boy" mean two very different things.

In Latin there is more flexibility when it comes to word order. The five sentences *puer pulsat murum, puer murum pulsat, murum puer pulsat, pulsat murum puer,* and *pulsat puer murum* all describe the same scene where the boy is punching the wall. None of the sentences is ambiguous as to what is being punched. Even the third example where the word for "wall" is placed at the beginning is clear. The wall is being punched in every example because it has the accusative ending, *-um* for the direct object.

This flexible word order is foreign to English, so a lot of Latin curricula end up using a standard word order to help young students. Since all our sentences are illustrated, we will be able to use different orders without causing any confusion. For sentences with direct objects we will often use this order: subject, direct object, verb. But if a student changes the order and still gets the endings correct, the sentence is not actually wrong. In fact, it is a good exercise to have the students say or write out the same sentence in different orders.

Much of what we've talked about in this lesson is a little abstract and can be difficult for some young students to grasp. However, the concept of direct object is extremely important in Latin and needs to be reviewed regularly. For several weeks, when the students are looking at a sentence with a direct object, ask them *why* the word is in the accusative and what direct object actually means. Have them rewrite Latin sentences in different orders on a personal whiteboard to reinforce that word order does not change meaning in Latin.

Regulae

- *direct object* - a word that someone is doing the verb to
- A direct object always goes in the accusative case.

Tabulae (Traditional Order)

CASE	FUNCTION	SG.	PL.
Normal		US	I
Accusative	After prepositions *ad, ante, post, super, and apud* **As a direct object**	UM	
Ablative	After prepositions *in, cum, ab, ex,* and *sub*	O	

Tabulae (British Order)

CASE	FUNCTION	SG.	PL.
Normal		US	I
Accusative	After prepositions *ad, ante, post, super, and apud* **As a direct object**	UM	
Ablative	After prepositions *in, cum, ab, ex,* and *sub*	O	

Lesson 8

Vocabula

- *deus* - god; this was used both for the Greco-Roman gods and for the Judeo-Christian God
- *medicus* - doctor
- *nuntius* - messenger
- *pullus* - chick; this was sometimes used of other animals too
- *umerus* - shoulder
- *focus* - cooktop; this word is sometimes translated as "hearth"--it was an open fire in the house

Lesson: Dative Case & Indirect Object

The indirect object is a second kind of object that often answers the question "to whom?". In the English sentence, "The boy gives the food to the master", the word "master" is the indirect object. In Latin, an indirect object changes to a new case called the dative case. An -*us* word changes to -*o* in the dative case. This seems like it would get confused with the ablative, but it is not as confusing as you might think. The dative case never appears after a preposition in Latin.

It is a bit tricky at first to say, "The boy gives food to the master." After all, we now have to change one word into the accusative case and another into the dative case. *Cibus* will be the direct object (answering "what does the boy give"), so it will become accusative and take an -*um* as its ending: *cibum*. *Dominus* will be the indirect object (answering "to whom does he give the food") and will become dative and take an -*o* as its ending: *domino*. Translating the whole sentence into Latin we get, *Puer dat cibum domino* (the boy gives the food to the master).

It would be a good idea to walk the students through many examples in the grammar exercises in the following way:

Teacher: "What's this sentence?"
Students: "*Puer domino cibum dat.*"
Teacher: "What case is *cibum*?"
Students: "Accusative"
Teacher: "Why is *cibum* accusative?"
Students: "It is the direct object."
Teacher: "Why is it the direct object?
Students: "Because it answers the question, *What is the boy giving*?"
Teacher: "What case is *domino*?
Students: "Dative"
Teacher: "Why is *domino* in the dative case?
Students: "Because it is the indirect object."
Teacher: "Why is it the indirect object?"
Students: "Because it is answering the question, "To whom is the boy giving food?"

There are few things in Latin grammar as important as the concepts of the direct and indirect object. Whenever you encounter a sentence with a direct object and indirect object, quiz the students in this way until it is solidified in their minds.

Word order in Latin is flexible. Sentences in this course tend to use the following order: subject, indirect object, direct object, verb. In that order we say, *Puer domino cibum dat.* Since word order can change so drastically in Latin, have your students rewrite one sentence in many different orders from time to time. Every once in a while when a sentence with a direct object and indirect object comes up in the app-based exercises, have the students write the sentence out on a personal whiteboard. Then, when a student has done it correctly in the normal order, ask them to rearrange it a couple times.

It may seem like this lesson is much more difficult than the preceding lessons. Students will now have to deal with direct objects and indirect objects and must remember what endings they take. In reality, this lesson is not too difficult because of the method we employ. By memorizing so many examples, the concepts of direct object and indirect object will quickly begin to make sense.

Regulae

- *indirect object* - a second kind of object that often answers the question *to whom?*
- *dative case* - a new case that it used for the indirect object
- An indirect object always goes in the dative case.
- The verb *dat* takes an indirect object for the person or thing to whom someone gives something.
- A word ending in *-us* usually turns to *-o* in the dative case.
- Ablative and dative sometimes look alike but they are not the same.

Tabulae (Traditional Order)

CASE	FUNCTION	SG.	PL.
Normal		US	I
Dative	**Indirect Object**	**O**	
Accusative	After prepositions *ad, ante, post, super,* and *apud* As a direct object	UM	
Ablative	After prepositions *in, cum, ab, ex,* and *sub*	O	

Tabulae (British Order)

CASE	FUNCTION	SG.	PL.
Normal		US	I
Accusative	After prepositions *ad, ante, post, super,* and *apud* As a direct object	UM	
Dative	**Indirect Object**	**O**	
Ablative	After prepositions *in, cum, ab, ex,* and *sub*	O	

Lesson 9

Vocabula

- *nidus* - nest; this word especially refers to birds' nests, but it can refer to other animals' homes
- *numerus* - number
- *oceanus* - ocean; this is not the usual word for "ocean" or "sea", but it is the easiest
- *ramus* - branch
- *rivus* - stream
- *tyrannus* - tyrant; one with absolute power, often thought of a harsh and cruel

- *quot?* - how many?; use this to ask for a counting number such as *unus, duo,* or *tres*
- *unus* - one; later on you may see this word with a different ending
- *duo* - two; later on you may see this word with a different ending
- *tres* - three; later on you may see this word with a different ending

Lesson: Genitive Case

This lesson is about how to show possession in Latin, answering the question "whose?". To show possession, Latin uses a case ending on the noun that is doing the "possessing". In English we do something similar. We say, "the **servant's** food" (notice the apostrophe and s). In Latin, we use a new case called the genitive case. *-U*s words generally change to *-i* in the genitive case. So *cibus servi* would mean "the servant's food". The word *servi* is in the genitive case.

Your students will immediately recognize that this ending is not unique--they have seen it before. They learned the *-i* ending in the very first lesson for the plural of the normal form. This is actually similar to English, where "dog's" is possessive, but "dogs" is plural. So how can we tell whether a word is plural or genitive? In difficult Latin we are often forced to rely solely on context. However, in this course the examples are very basic, and the illustrations make them obvious. Pictures showing possession will have a character pointing to himself and either holding or pointing to the thing he is possessing. The character pointing to himself, since he is possessing, will always be the noun that takes the genitive ending. For instance, when there is a servant pointing to himself the students will answer with "*servi*"; when there is a wolf pointing to himself, they will answer "*lupi*". This is like saying "the servant's" and the "wolf's" in English.

The sentences in the app-based exercises will generally follow this order: thing possessed, then one who "possesses" it. So, the translation we saw before, "the servant's food", will be expressed as *cibus servi*.

One final note. In lesson 7 we encountered the verb *habet*. The difference between pictures which are answered with *habet* and those which are answered with the possessive *-i* is very slight. If someone in the picture is pointing to himself, answer with the possessive *-i*. If no one is pointing, answer with *habet*. This is, of course, just for the purpose of the exercise. In real Latin, one could express the idea either way. It would be like saying, "The wolf has food" or "the wolf's food". Each way expresses possession in a different way.

Regulae

- *genitive case* - a new case that can answer the question *whose?*
- A word that ends in *-us* usually changes to an *-i* in the genitive case.
- The genitive ending *-i* looks like the plural ending *-i*, but they are not the same.

Tabulae (Traditional Order)

US

CASE	FUNCTION	SG.	PL.
Normal		US	I
Genitive	**Possession**	**I**	
Dative	Indirect Object	O	
Accusative	After prepositions *ad, ante, post, super,* and *apud* As a direct object	UM	
Ablative	After prepositions *in, cum, ab, ex,* and *sub*	O	

Tabulae (British Order)

US

CASE	FUNCTION	SG.	PL.
Normal		US	I
Accusative	After prepositions *ad, ante, post, super,* and *apud* As a direct object	UM	
Genitive	**Possession**	**I**	
Dative	Indirect Object	O	
Ablative	After prepositions *in, cum, ab, ex,* and *sub*	O	

Lesson 10

Vocabula

- *vir* - man; this specifically means a male adult--not just a human being
- *clipeus* - shield; this is a round shield--there is a different word for a rectangular shield
- *discipulus* - student
- *pugnus* - fist
- *ludus* - school; this refers to younger children who are learning reading, writing, and arithmetic
- *colonus* - farmer; this is specifically a poor farmer who rents land from a landlord

- *quid?* - what?
- *nullus* - not any

Lesson: Nominative Case

Whenever you learn a new noun like *puer*, you learn it in a case called the nominative case (literally, "the naming case"). Up until this point, we have always just called this the "normal" form to avoid using too much technical terminology too early on. From now on, we will call it the nominative case. The nominative case is used for the subject of a sentence. What is a subject? It is the noun that the sentence (and especially the verb of the sentence) is about. If the students have not already done this, have them write the singular and plural forms of the nominative case in their student workbooks for *-us* words.

Regulae

- *subject* - the word that the verb of a sentence is about
- *nominative* - the "normal" case of a word, used for the subject
- The subject of a sentence is put in the nominative case.

Tabulae (Traditional Order)

US

CASE	FUNCTION	SG.	PL.
Nominative	**Subject**	US	I
Genitive	Possession	I	
Dative	Indirect Object	O	
Accusative	After prepositions *ad, ante, post, super,* and *apud* As a direct object	UM	
Ablative	After prepositions *in, cum, ab, ex,* and *sub*	O	

Tabulae (British Order)

US

CASE	FUNCTION	SG.	PL.
Nominative	**Subject**	US	I
Accusative	After prepositions *ad, ante, post, super,* and *apud* As a direct object	UM	
Genitive	Possession	I	
Dative	Indirect Object	O	
Ablative	After prepositions *in, cum, ab, ex,* and *sub*	O	

Lesson: -Er Words

In this lesson your students will learn how to use two extremely important words: *puer* and *vir*. *Puer* and *vir* are -*er* words--words that work almost exactly like -*us* words. *Puer* and *vir* both the exact same endings that all our -*us* words have. But unlike normal -*us* words, there is nothing to remove before you add an ending. So the ablative of *puer* is *puero*.

So, after the prepositions *in, cum, ab, sub,* and *ex*: *puer* and *vir* change to *puero* and *viro*. After *ad, ante, post, super,* and *apud*: they change to *puerum* and *virum*. When they are the direct object of the sentence our words become *puerum* and *virum*. When they are the indirect object of the sentence, they become *puero* and *viro*. When either of these two nouns is possessing something, they become *pueri* and *viri*. And finally, when there are two or more of these things in the nominative case, the words become *pueri* and *viri*.

Regulae

- Words that end in *-er* usually get the same endings as *-us* words.

Tabulae (Traditional Order)

ER

CASE	FUNCTION	SG.	PL.
Nominative	Subject	ER	I
Genitive	Possession	I	
Dative	Indirect Object	O	
Accusative	After prepositions *ad*, *ante*, *post*, *super*, and *apud* As a direct object	UM	
Ablative	After prepositions *in*, *cum*, *ab*, *ex*, and *sub*	O	

Tabulae (British Order)

ER

CASE	FUNCTION	SG.	PL.
Nominative	Subject	ER	I
Accusative	After prepositions *ad*, *ante*, *post*, *super*, and *apud* As a direct object	UM	
Genitive	Possession	I	
Dative	Indirect Object	O	
Ablative	After prepositions *in*, *cum*, *ab*, *ex*, and *sub*	O	

Lesson 11

Vocabula

- *liber* - book; a Roman book was usually in the form of a scroll
- *magister* - teacher; this word was used for anyone who kept people in line
- *minister* - waiter; this referred to servants that brought food to their masters' tables
- *ager* - field; this is specifically the kind of field where crops or fruit trees were grown
- *culter* - knife
- *aper* - boar

- *neque* - and not
- *quattuor* - four
- *quinque* - five
- *ecce* - look; this is an interjection used to draw attention to something--use when pointing

Lesson: *Er*-Words Dropping E

In this lesson your students will learn five more -*er* words. But these words lose the letter *e* before the *r* whenever they change their endings. With *puer* and *vir* all your students had to do was add the appropriate ending. Our five new words require the same adjustment but only after you have gotten rid of an *e*.

Ager is one of the five words we will be exercising in this lesson. After the preposition *in*, *ager* becomes *agro*. The word gets an -*o* ending just like all our other -*us* words but notice that the *e* from the original word has dropped out.

Here is what *ager* would look like in all the cases we have learned. In the ablative case, it becomes *agro*. In the accusative, it changes to *agrum*. In the dative case, it becomes *agro*. In the genitive case, it becomes *agri*. And in the nominative, plural, it becomes *agri*.

Regulae

- Words that end in -*er* usually get the same endings as -*us* words.
- Words that end in -*er* often lose the *e* when an ending is added.

Lesson 12

Vocabula

- *baculum* - stick; this is usually the kind of stick one uses to walk with--a staff
- *oppidum* - town
- *saxum* - rock; this is usually a rather large rock, like a boulder or crag
- *aedificium* - building
- *bracchium* - arm
- *collum* - neck
- *tergum* - back

Lesson: -*Um* Words

Up until this point, your students have been focusing on what we have called -*us* words (what grammarians call 2nd-declension masculine nouns). In this lesson your students will begin learning "-*um* words" (2nd-declension neuter nouns). It is not necessary at this point to introduce the technical name, so in *Picta Dicta Latin Primer* they will just be called -*um* words for the present. Volume 1 of this course does *not* introduce the concept of grammatical gender (i.e., the difference between masculine and neuter), so there is no need to bring this up with your students at this point either.

-*Um* words work like -*us* words except for in the nominative and accusative cases. This is why Latin grammarians have placed both of these groups into what they call the 2nd declension, a group of nouns that have a lot of *u* and *o* in their endings. But again, this is not important (or even helpful) for your students to learn at this point. In this lesson, your students simply learn that an -*um* word has the ending -*um* when it is in the nominative case. So in *Aedificium in oppido est*, the word *aedificium* is nominative--not accusative. If your students really got the concept that -*um* means accusative and direct object, this new rule may give them some trouble. This is completely normal. You must impress upon them that -*um* words work differently than -*us* words in this respect. It may be necessary to do a little extra drilling when you are introducing vocabulary for the next couple lessons:

Teacher: "What's this new word?"
Students: "*Oppidum*!"
Teacher: "What kind of word is this?"
Students:; "An -*um* word!"
Teacher: "What's the nominative of *oppidum*?"
Students: "*Oppidum*!"

Your students will also learn in this lesson that -*um* words change to -*o* in the ablative case--this is no different than with -*us* words. Be sure to point out this similarity frequently.

Students will practice using -*um* words with the prepositions *in, cum, ab, sub,* and *ex*. This is a great time to review which prepositions take the ablative case and which take the accusative case. It is helpful to have the students chant out which prepositions take the ablative from time to time:

Teacher: "Which prepositions take the ablative?"
Students: "*In, cum, ab, sub, ex*, and a few more we haven't learned!"
Teacher: "What case do the prepositions that don't take ablative take?"
Students: "Accusative!"

Regulae

- Words that end in *-um* in the nominative case are a new kind of word.
- The ending of an *-um* word changes to *-o* in the ablative case.

Tabulae (Traditional & British Order)

UM

CASE	FUNCTION	SG.	PL.
Nominative	**Subject**	**UM**	
Ablative	**After prepositions *in*, *cum*, *ab*, *ex*, and *sub***	**O**	

Lesson 13

Vocabula

- *astrum* - star
- *caelum* - sky; this word is also used to mean "heaven"
- *cubiculum* - bedroom
- *scutum* - shield; this kind of shield is rectangular unlike the round *clipeus*
- *telum* - javelin; this word can also refer to other thrown weapons
- *vinum* - wine
- *poculum* - cup

- *unde*? - from where?; students will often answer this question with *ab* or *ex* and an ablative

Lesson: *-Um* Words in the Accusative

-Um words in the accusative case end in *-um*, just like they do in the nominative case. This means that you can only tell if an *-um* word is nominative or accusative by context. In this lesson, *-um* words will appear as the object of prepositions that take the accusative case, such as *ad*, *ante*, *post*, *super*, and *apud*. A good exercise when going through the sentences is to quiz students on the case and function of the *-um* words--even when it has to be determined by context.

Sentence: *Aedificium super saxum est.*
Teacher: "What case is *saxum*?"
Students: "Accusative!"
Teacher: "How do you know? Couldn't it also be nominative since it is an *-um* word?"
Students: "It goes with the preposition *super*, which takes the accusative case."
Teacher: "What case is *aedificium*?"
Students: "Nominative!"
Teacher: "How do you know? Couldn't it also be accusative since it is an *-um* word?"
Students: "It is the subject of the sentence, so it has to be nominative."

Regulae

- An *-um* word always looks the same in the nominative and the accusative: *-um*.

Tabulae (Traditional Order)

UM

CASE	FUNCTION	SG.	PL.
Nominative	Subject	UM	
Accusative	**After prepositions *ad, ante, post, super,* and *apud*** **As a direct object**	UM	
Ablative	After prepositions *in, cum, ab, ex,* and *sub*	O	

Tabulae (British Order)

UM

CASE	FUNCTION	SG.	PL.
Nominative	Subject	UM	
Accusative	**After prepositions *ad, ante, post, super,* and *apud*** **As a direct object**	UM	
Ablative	After prepositions *in, cum, ab, ex,* and *sub*	O	

Lesson 14

Vocabula

- *sumit* - picks up
- *ponit* - puts
- *iacit* - throws
- *capit* - catches
- *malum* - apple
- *pirum* - pear
- *donum* - present

- *quo?* - where to?; students often answer this question with *ad* and the accusative case

Be sure the students understand the difference between *capit* and *iacit*, and *sumit* and *ponit*. The motion blur shows how each action works, but it is a good idea to point it out to the students as a class to make sure they understand.

Lesson: *-Um* Words as Direct Objects

In this lesson your students continue to learn to use *-um* words in the accusative case, but this time they will see them as direct objects. This is a little more difficult because there is no preposition to make it clear that the *-um* word is accusative. The best way to help them learn to recognize an *-um* word as a direct object is to walk them through the process with questions and answers:

Example: *Puer malum iacit.*
Teacher: "What case is *malum*?"
Students: "Accusative."
Teacher: "How do you know it is not nominative? *Malum* is an *-um* word."
Students: "Because *malum* cannot be the subject of *iacit*--it does not make any sense. How would an apple do the throwing? Also, the sentence already has a nominative subject: *puer*."

In this lesson's vocabulary your students will learn four more verbs that can take direct objects: *ponit, sumit, iacit,* and *capit.* When a sentence has one of these verbs, they should learn to expect a direct object.

In lesson seven your students learned that word order is malleable in Latin. In this lesson your students will start seeing examples of different word orders. They have always given example sentences in this order: subject, object, verb. They may now encounter a new order: object, subject, verb.

Regulae

- An *-um* word as a direct object is in the accusative case and looks just like the nominative subject.

Lesson 15

Vocabula

- *aurum* - gold
- *argentum* - silver
- *bellum* - war
- *folium* - leaf
- *ovum* - egg
- *tectum* - roof
- *speculum* - mirror

Lesson: *-Um* Words in the Dative

In this lesson your students will learn to use *-um* words as indirect objects (in the dative case). Just like with *-us* words, *-um* words get the ending *-o* in the dative case. So *Puer oppido cibum dat*, would mean "The boy gives food to the town." This is a very easy lesson because the students have already come to think of *-o* as dative, so this is a great time to do some review. Take a few example sentences and quiz the students on the cases for all the nouns.

Example: *Puer oppido cibum dat.*
Teacher: "What case is *puer*?"
Students: "Nominative!"
Teacher: "Why is it nominative?"
Students: "It is the subject of the sentence--the puer is doing the giving."
Teacher: "What case is *cibum*?"
Students: "Accusative!"
Teacher: "Why is it accusative?"
Students: "It is the direct object--it answers what the *puer* is giving."
Teacher: "What case is *oppido*?"
Students: "Dative!"
Teacher: "Why is it dative?"
Students: "It is the indirect object--it answers to whom is the puer giving the *cibus*."

In this lesson your students will continue to see sentences that are in a different word order: indirect object, subject, object, verb (*Domino puer cibum dat.*) The order, of course, makes no difference to the meaning of the sentence, but sometimes students will struggle at first when they see a new order. *Domino puer cibum dat* means the same thing as *Puer domino cibum dat*. Both would be translated "The boy gives food to the master". When you encounter an example like this, take the time to quiz your students on the cases and functions of all the nouns.

Example: *Domino puer cibum dat.*
Teacher: "What case is *domino*?"
Students: "Dative!"
Teacher: "What? It is the first word in the sentence. Isn't it nominative?"
Students: "No. The ending is *-o*, and the word dat needs a dative in the sentence."

Regulae

- An *-um* word changes its ending to *-o* in the dative case.

Tabulae (Traditional Order)

UM

CASE	FUNCTION	SG.	PL.
Nominative	Subject	UM	
Dative	**Indirect Object**	**O**	
Accusative	After prepositions *ad, ante, post, super, and apud* As a direct object	UM	
Ablative	After prepositions *in, cum, ab, ex,* and *sub*	O	

Tabulae (British Order)

UM

CASE	FUNCTION	SG.	PL.
Nominative	Subject	UM	
Accusative	After prepositions *ad, ante, post, super, and apud* As a direct object	UM	
Dative	**Indirect Object**	**O**	
Ablative	After prepositions *in, cum, ab, ex,* and *sub*	O	

Lesson 16

Vocabula

- *monstrum* - monster
- *vestigium* - track
- *ostium* - door;
- *balneum* - bathtub; this can also mean the bath itself
- *lignum* - wood
- *vocabulum* - word

- *cur*? - why?
- *quia* - because

Lesson: *-Um* Words in the Genitive

In this lesson your students will see *-um* words in the genitive case, showing possession. The genitive of an *-um* word is *-i* just like it is for an *-us* word, so this is an easy lesson. In lesson nine your students learned that "the master's sword" is translated *gladius domini*. Similarly, the "monster's sword" is translated *gladius monstri*.

In this lesson your students will continue to see variation in word order. Sometimes you will see a sentence with the genitive first before the nominative: *domini gladius* instead of *gladius domini*. This makes no difference to the meaning, but it may cause some confusion at first. Just like with other variation in word order, take the opportunity to quiz the students on the cases. Ask them *how* they know which word is which. The skill of determining the ending ultimately makes the difference whether a student can read Latin or not, so any time spent drilling them is well spent.

Example: *domini gladius*
Teacher: "What case is *domini*?"
Students: "Genitive!"
Teacher: "What? That's crazy. It's the first word in the sentence. Don't you mean nominative?"
Students: "No, the ending shows that it is genitive. Also there is another word *gladius* that is clearly the nominative."
Teacher: "Hmm. You all may be right."

Regulae

- An *-um* word in the genitive case has the ending *-i*.

Tabulae (Traditional Order)

UM

CASE	FUNCTION	SG.	PL.
Nominative	Subject	UM	
Genitive	**Possession**	**I**	
Dative	Indirect Object	O	
Accusative	After prepositions *ad, ante, post, super, and apud* As a direct object	UM	
Ablative	After prepositions *in, cum, ab, ex,* and *sub*	O	

Tabulae (British Order)

UM

CASE	FUNCTION	SG.	PL.
Nominative	Subject	UM	
Accusative	After prepositions *ad, ante, post, super, and apud* As a direct object	UM	
Genitive	**Possession**	**I**	
Dative	Indirect Object	O	
Ablative	After prepositions *in, cum, ab, ex,* and *sub*	O	

Lesson 17

Vocabula

- *triclinium* - dining room
- *cerebrum* - brain
- *osculum* - kiss
- *labrum* - lip
- *vestimentum* - clothes
- *templum* - temple

Lesson: *-Um* words in the Nominative Plural

Up until this point, *-us* words and *-um* words have worked pretty much the same way, except for in the nominative case. In the nominative plural, *-um* words will again look different from *-us* words: instead of getting the ending *-i*, they get the ending *-a*. So *oppidum* means "town", but *oppida* means "towns".

This is also true of some words that have come from Latin into English, like *curriculum* and *datum*. But comparisons like these rarely help elementary students very much! The best way to get students to understand this is by guiding them through the process of turning different kinds of words into the nominative plural from time to time.

Teacher: "What would *monstrum* be in the plural?"
Students: "*Monstra*!"
Teacher: "Why not *monstri*?"
Students: "Because *monstrum* is an *-um* word, not an *-us* word."
Teacher: "What about *stilus* in the plural? What is that?"
Students: "*Stili*!"
Teacher: "Wait a minute! Shouldn't it be *stila*?"
Students: "No. Stilus is an *-us* word, so the plural is *stili*."
Teacher: "Sheesh. Latin is tricky, isn't it?"

Est and *Sunt*

Your students have already been seeing singular and plural words for quite a while, but in this lesson they will see plural verbs for the first time. If the subject of a sentence is plural, the verb of that sentence should be plural as well. So if *pueri* is the subject of a sentence, the verb *est* will need to become plural as well. *Sunt* is the plural of *est*, just like *are* is the plural of *is* in English.

Example: *Pueri in horto sunt.*
Teacher: "What number is *pueri*?"
Students: "Plural!"
Teacher: "How do you know?"
Students: "It has the nominative plural ending, *-i*!"
Teacher: "What is this *sunt* word doing in the sentence?"
Students: "It is the plural of *est*."
Teacher: "Why does *sunt* need to be plural?"
Students: "Because the subject *pueri* is plural and the verb matches the subject."

Regulae

- An *-um* word in the nominative plural changes to *-a*.
- A verb must be plural if its subject is plural.
- The plural of *est* is *sunt*.

Tabulae (Traditional Order)

UM

CASE	FUNCTION	SG.	PL.
Nominative	Subject	UM	**A**
Genitive	Possession	I	
Dative	Indirect Object	O	
Accusative	After prepositions *ad, ante, post, super, and apud* As a direct object	UM	
Ablative	After prepositions *in, cum, ab, ex,* and *sub*	O	

Tabulae (British Order)

UM

CASE	FUNCTION	SG.	PL.
Nominative	Subject	UM	**A**
Accusative	After prepositions *ad, ante, post, super, and apud* As a direct object	UM	
Genitive	Possession	I	
Dative	Indirect Object	O	
Ablative	After prepositions *in, cum, ab, ex,* and *sub*	O	

Lesson 18

Vocabula

- *puella* - girl
- *femina* - woman
- *insula* - island
- *villa* - house; this is especially a country house with a farm attached
- *sella* - chair; a real Roman sella had no arms or back
- *mensa* - table; Roman tables were often round with three legs
- *via* - road; Roman roads were paved with stones

- *de* - about; this word also can mean "down from" if the context is about movement

Lesson: -*A* Words

The first word your students learned in this course was *puer*. Perhaps all the girls in the class have been wondering ever since when they were going to learn the word for "girl". In lesson 18, it is finally time! Your students have not learned the word for *girl* (or any other females) yet because such words are neither -*us* words nor -*um* words in Latin. Instead, they are -*a* words, a new kind of noun that we will be focusing on for the next five lessons. If you are already familiar with Latin, you will recognize these as 1st-declension nouns. Most textbooks begin with this kind of word simply because they are the *1st* declension and *a* is the first letter in the alphabet. However, since -*us* words and -*um* words (called 2nd-declension nouns by grammarians) are so similar to each other, we teach them first in this course.

-*A* words are trickier than -*us* or -*um* words because the nominative and ablative case look almost identical. The nominative singular form is just -*a* (pronounced *ah*), but the ablative case is -*ā* (pronounced *aah*--the very same sound, but drawn out about 50% longer). The bar above the letter *a* in the ablative is called a macron. This symbol shows that a vowel is pronounced longer than it normally would be. There are actually macrons in many Latin words and endings that your students have already learned in this course. But do not be dismayed! It is not at all necessary to memorize the vast majority of the macrons in Latin--unless you decide to start writing poetry in Latin. Only a few of them make a difference in meaning. These are the only important ones to remember, and chief among them is the ablative ending -*ā*. When your students compose a Latin sentence, make sure that they remember to write the macron over the *a* to make it ablative--consider it part of the spelling. When they forget it (which they will frequently), say something like, "Aren't you forgetting something...loooong that goes over some letters sometimes?"

When your students pronounce an -*a* word in the ablative case aloud, make sure that they lengthen the sound at the end. It is fun to exaggerate its length a bit at first to make the point.

In this lesson your students will be working with the prepositions *in, cum, ab, sub,* and *ex*. They will also learn a new preposition: *de. De* works in the same way as these other five prepositions it takes a word in the ablative case as its object: for example, *Puer de insulā cogitat.*

Lesson B: -*A* Words in the Nominative Plural

Your students will also learn how to make -*a* words plural. The ending on an -*a* word changes to *ae* (pronounced like "eye") when it is plural. There is one *puella*, but two or more *puellae*.

The letter combination *ae* is always pronounced as one sound in Latin ("eye"). Many students hear that sound and want to spell it with the English letter *-i*. It may be necessary to drill your students with the two spellings so that they do not get confused. Call out the sound "eeee", and have them write *i*. Then call out the sound "eye", and have them write *ae*.

Regulae

- *macron* - A macron is a line above a vowel that shows it should be pronounced longer.
- *-A* words are words that end in *-a* in the nominative, singular.
- An *-a* word's ending changes to *-ā* in the ablative case.
- *-A* words in the nominative plural get the ending *-ae*.

Tabulae (Traditional & British Order)

A

CASE	FUNCTION	SG.	PL.
Nominative	**Subject**	**A**	**AE**
Ablative	**After prepositions *in, cum, ab, ex, sub, de***	**Ā**	

53

Lesson 19

Vocabula

- *filia* - daughter
- *familia* - family; for Romans this meant everyone in the house, even servants
- *domina* - mistress; this was the lady of the house
- *lingua* - tongue; this word also means "language"
- *luna* - moon
- *ianua* - door
- *porta* - gate

- *per* - through

- *quis?* - who?

Lesson: *-A* Words in the Accusative

In this lesson your students will learn that an *-a* word gets the ending *-am* in the accusative case. Make sure to point out to your students that there is an *m* in the *-um* and the *-am* accusative endings. This comparison should help them remember the form.

This lesson will focus on the prepositions that take the accusative case: *ad, ante, post, super,* and *apud.* Your students will learn a new preposition that also takes the accusative: *per.* This is a great time to have your students practice listing these out as well as those that take the ablative case.

Teacher: "What prepositions do you know that take the accusative case?"
Students: "*Ad, ante, post, super, apud*, and *per.*"
Teacher: "What prepositions do you know that take the ablative case?"
Students: "*In, cum, ab, ex, sub*, and *de*"
Teacher: "If you didn't remember which case goes with a preposition, which one would be better to guess."
Students: "Accusative because most prepositions take the accusative case."

Another useful drill is to call out a preposition and have the students write which case it takes: ablative or accusative. This can be done as a group orally or individually on personal whiteboards.

Teacher: "*Cum.*"
Students: "Ablative!"
Teacher: "*Ante.*"
Students: "Accusative!"
Teacher: "*Super.*"
Students: "Accusative!"
Teacher: "*Sub*"
Students: "Ablative!"

Another good drill to practice the accusative is to write a preposition on the board like *per*. Have the students complete the phrase with a word in the accusative case so that it makes sense. Ideally, the teacher should comment on the students' examples. This can be done orally or on personal whiteboards, depending on the time.

Example: *per*
Student 1: "*per fluvium*"
Teacher: "Good, but very wet"
Student 2: "*per hortum*"
Teacher: "Good grammar; bad idea. Your mom will get after you if you go *per hortum*."
Student 3: "*per nasum*"
Teacher: "Hmm. That works, but isn't pleasant to think about."
Student 4: "*per bellum*"
Teacher: "Sounds dangerous."
Student 5: "*per lunam*"
Teacher: "That would be difficult."

Regulae

♦ An *-a* word changes its ending to *-am* in the accusative case.

Tabulae (Traditional Order)

A

CASE	FUNCTION	SG.	PL.
Nominative	Subject	A	AE
Accusative	**Direct Object** **After prepositions** *ad*, *ante*, *post*, *super*, *apud*, **and** *per*	**AM**	
Ablative	After prepositions *in*, *cum*, *ab*, *ex*, *sub*, *de*	Ā	

Tabulae (British Order)

A

CASE	FUNCTION	SG.	PL.
Nominative	Subject	A	AE
Accusative	**Direct Object** **After prepositions** *ad*, *ante*, *post*, *super*, *apud*, **and** *per*	**AM**	
Ablative	After prepositions *in*, *cum*, *ab*, *ex*, *sub*, *de*	Ā	

Lesson 20

Vocabula

- *plorat* - cries
- *ridet* - laughs
- *amat* - loves
- *currit* - runs
- *fert* - carries
- *timet* - fears

Lesson: -*A* Words as Direct Objects

In this lesson your students see -a words used as direct objects of verbs. In addition to the verbs you have already seen, this chapter introduces eight new verbs. Of these, *amat*, *fert*, and *timet* will take direct objects in the example. A teacher can never review the difference between subject and direct object enough. This lesson is not very difficult because there are no new rules, so it is a great time to review subjects and objects.

A great exercise to drill the direct object (and accusative) is to write part of a sentence on the board where the direct object is missing. Have students supply the missing word in the accusative case. This can be done orally or on personal whiteboards. Ideally, the teacher should make comments on the students' examples.

Example: *Monstrum* _____ *timet.*
Teacher: "What is missing from this sentence?"
Students: "Direct Object."
Teacher: "Good! What case should the direct object be in?"
Students: "Accusative."
Teacher: "Excellent. What is the accusative ending for an -*us* word?"
Students: "-*um*".
Teacher: "What is the accusative ending for an -*um* word?"
Students: "-*um*".
Teacher: "What is the accusative ending for an -*a* word?"
Students: "-*am*".
Teacher: "Excellent! So let's fill in that blank!"
Student 1: "*Calceum!*"
Teacher: "Wow. Really? What kind of self-respecting *monstrum* is afraid of a shoe?"
Student 2: "*Puerum!*"
Teacher: "Interesting. So it goes both ways then?"
Student 3: "*Insulam!*"
Teacher: "Good. Sounds like there is a good story there."

Lesson 21

Vocabula

- *epistula* - letter
- *rosa* - rose
- *pila* - ball
- *pagina* - page
- *regina* - queen
- *corona* - crown
- *flamma* - flame

Lesson: *-A* Words in the Dative

In this lesson your students will learn that the dative case ending for an *-a* word is *-ae*. This looks like the nominative plural ending, so it will be necessary for the students to learn to pay close attention to the context. The dative case is not going to show up in a sentence unless it needs something like an indirect object. In this course a sentence will only need an indirect object if the verb is *dat*. Later on, students will see that other verbs may require a dative, but for now they need to come to expect an indirect object with *dat*.

The indirect object is a difficult concept for young students to remember, so it is usually best to teach them that it sometimes answers the question *to whom something is given*. Since this chapter is revisiting the indirect object, it is the perfect time to reinforce the difference between the direct object (*what the subject is doing something to*) and the indirect object (*to whom is the subject giving something*).

Example: *Nuntius feminae epistulam dat.*
Teacher: "Okay, which one of these words is the subject of the sentence?"
Students: "*Nuntius*!"
Teacher: "Good. Why?"
Students: "It is in the nominative case--it ends in *-us*!"
Teacher: "Good. What is the subject doing in this sentence?"
Students: "*Dat*." or "He is giving".
Teacher: "Good. What is the *nuntius* giving?"
Students: "*Epistulam*!" or "The letter."
Teacher: "Good. How do you know he is giving the *epistulam*?"
Students: "That is the direct object--it is in the accusative case. It ends in *-am*!"
Teacher: "What about this word *feminae*? What case is it?"
Students: "Dative!"
Teacher: "How do you know it is not nominative plural? It ends in *-ae*, you know."
Students: "We already have a subject *nuntius*, and the verb *dat* usually needs an indirect object."
Teacher: "You all are so smart."

Regulae

- An *-a* word in the dative has the ending *-ae*.

Tabulae (Traditional Order)

A

CASE	FUNCTION	SG.	PL.
Nominative	Subject	A	AE
Dative	**Indirect Object**	**AE**	
Accusative	Direct Object After prepositions *ad, ante, post, super, apud,* and *per*	AM	
Ablative	After prepositions *in, cum, ab, ex, sub, de*	Ā	

Tabulae (British Order)

A

CASE	FUNCTION	SG.	PL.
Nominative	Subject	A	AE
Accusative	Direct Object After prepositions *ad, ante, post, super, apud,* and *per*	AM	
Dative	**Indirect Object**	**AE**	
Ablative	After prepositions *in, cum, ab, ex, sub, de*	Ā	

Lesson 22

Vocabula

- *aqua* - water
- *fenestra* - window
- *tabula* - board
- *dea* - goddess
- *cauda* - tail
- *aquila* - eagle
- *penna* - feather

Lesson: *-A* Words in the Genitive Case

In this lesson your students will learn that the genitive case for an *-a* word is *-ae*. This is a bit tricky at first because now they know three endings for *-a* words that are *-ae*: nominative plural, dative, and genitive. First you must get students to understand that *-ae* could be one of three endings. The student workbook and *sententiae* quizzes will bring this question up regularly, but it is good to reinforce it in class.

Once students understand that there are three possibilities, you must teach them to read the context and understand what a sentence needs to make sense. If the sentence already has a subject, the ending *-ae* is probably not nominative plural; if the sentence has the verb *dat*, the ending *-ae* is probably dative; if the ending *-ae* is on a word that makes sense answering the question *whose*, it is probably genitive. This kind of reasoning from context is often challenging for elementary students; however, if it is introduced step by step and regularly reinforced through drilling, even younger children can master it. When people talk about Latin helping students with reasoning, they are talking about this kind of contextual grammatical reasoning. It is hard work, but it is worth it! It is also best done as a group.

Example: *calcei puellae*
Teacher: "What case is *puellae*?"
Students: "Probably genitive."
Teacher: "Why do you think that?"
Students: "Because one of those words has to be nominative plural and the other has to be genitive."
Teacher: "Why couldn't *puellae* be dative?"
Students: "Because there is no verb like *dat* in the sentence."
Teacher: "Why do you think *puellae* is the genitive one and not the nominative plural?"
Students: "Because if it was the nominative plural, then *calcei* would be genitive. That would mean that there were some girls that belong to a shoe: "the shoe's girls"."
Teacher: "Hmm. I see your point. Good thinking!"

Example: *Puellae in horto sunt.*
Teacher: "What case is *puellae*?"
Students: "Probably nominative plural!"
Teacher: "Why do you say that?"
Students: "Nothing else in the sentence could be nominative, and the sentence needs a subject."
Teacher: "True. If *puellae* is the plural subject, what else needs to be plural?"
Students: "The verb."
Teacher: "Is *sunt* plural?"

Students: "Yes."
Teacher: "Good. Then *puellae* probably is the nominative subject."

Example: *Puer puellae gladium dat.*
Teacher: "What case is *puellae*?"
Students: "Probably dative."
Teacher: "Why do you say that?"
Students: "Because the sentence already has a nominative subject, *puer*, and the verb *dat* needs an indirect object."
Teacher: "Good. Why could it not be genitive?"
Students: "Well, if *puellae* is genitive, it would be answering *whose gladium*. That would be like saying, "The boy gives the girl's sword." It makes sense, but we still do not know *to whom the sword is given*. So, it is probably dative.
Teacher: "Wonderful."

Regulae

♦ *-A* words in the genitive case have the ending *-ae*.

Tabulae (Traditional Order)

A

CASE	FUNCTION	SG.	PL.
Nominative	Subject	A	AE
Genitive	**Possession**	**AE**	
Dative	Indirect Object	AE	
Accusative	Direct Object After prepositions *ad, ante, post, super, apud,* and *per*	AM	
Ablative	After prepositions *in, cum, ab, ex, sub, de*	Ā	

Tabulae (British Order)

A

CASE	FUNCTION	SG.	PL.
Nominative	Subject	A	AE
Accusative	Direct Object After prepositions *ad, ante, post, super, apud,* and *per*	AM	
Genitive	**Possession**	**AE**	
Dative	Indirect Object	AE	
Ablative	After prepositions *in, cum, ab, ex, sub, de*	Ā	

Lesson 23

Case Review

This lesson is designed for review: there are no new vocabulary, grammar rules, or forms to learn. Your students have now learned how to use all five cases of *-us* words, *-er* words, *-um* words, and *-a* words in the singular. This is quite a lot for an elementary student to hold in their head all at once; so before we move on to learning all the cases in the plural, it is important to make sure the students have the singular forms and concepts solid. Question and answer reviews are a good way to do this, but make sure not to review too much in one session. Here are some example review discussions that would be good to work in throughout the week.

Nominative Review:

Teacher: "What is the nominative case for?"
Students: "Subject"
Teacher: "What is a subject?"
Students: "It is the word that the sentence is about."
Teacher: "What does the nominative case look like for an *-us* word?"
Students: "*-us*"
Teacher: "Let's hear five examples of *-us* words in the nominative singular."
Students: "*lupus, stilus, pugnus, clipeus, campus.*"
Teacher: "Good! What does the nominative case look like for an *-us* word if it is plural?"
Students: "*-i*"
Teacher: "Let's hear five examples of *-us* words in the nominative plural."
Students: "*lupi, stili, pugni, clipei, campi*"
Teacher: "What does the nominative case look like for an *-er* word?
Students: "*-er*!"
Teacher: "Good. Let's hear five examples of *-er* words in the nominative singular."
Students: "*puer, ager, magister, minister, culter*"
Teacher: "Great! What does the nominative plural look like for an *-er* word?"
Students: "*-i*. The *-r* stays, but the *e* drops out most of the time."
Teacher: "Let's hear five examples of *-er* words in the nominative plural."
Students: "*pueri, agri, magistri, ministri, cultri*"
Teacher: "What does the nominative case look like in an *-um* word?"
Students: "*-um*"
Teacher: "Good. Let's hear five examples of *-um* words in the nominative singular."
Students: "*oppidum, baculum, folium, aedificium, astrum*"
Teacher: "What does an *-um* word look like in the nominative plural?"
Students: "*-a*"
Teacher: "Excellent! Give five examples of *-um* words in the nominative plural.
Students: "*oppida, bacula, folia, aedificia, astra*"
Teacher: "Well done. What does the nominative case look like in an *-a* word?
Students: "*-a*"
Teacher: "Give five examples of *-a* words in the nominative singular."
Students: "*puella, femina, sella, mensa, insula*"
Teacher: "What does an *-a* word look like in the nominative plural?"
Students: "*-ae*"

Teacher: "Give five examples of -a words in the nominative plural."
Students: "*puellae, feminae, sellae, mensae, insulae*"

Ablative Review:

Teacher: "When do you use the ablative case?
Students: "After certain prepositions."
Teacher: "Which prepositions have you learned that take the ablative case?"
Students: "*in, cum, ab, ex, sub,* and *de.*"
Teacher: "What does the ablative case look like in an -us word?
Students: "-o"
Teacher: "Give five examples of -us words in the ablative case.
Students: "*campo, lupo, fluvio, horto, gladio*"
Teacher: "Great! What does the ablative case look like in an -er word?"
Students: "-o. The -r stays but the e often drops out."
Teacher: "Good. Give me five examples of -er words in the ablative case."
Students: "*agro, cultro, magistro, ministro, puero*"
Teacher: "Wonderful. What does the ablative case look like in an -um word?"
Students: "-o"
Teacher: "Give five examples."
Students: "*oppido, aedificio, monstro, folio, saxo*"
Teacher: "Great. What does the ablative case look like in an -a word?"
Students: "-ā"
Teacher: "Why did you all say it like that?"
Students: "The ablative ending for an -a word is long--it has a macron."
Teacher: "What is a macron?"
Students: "A line above a vowel that means you are supposed to draw it out longer."
Teacher: "Give five examples of -a words in the ablative."
Students: "*puellā, feminā, mensā, sellā, insulā*"
Teacher: "Excellent work!"

Accusative Review:

Teacher: "What is the accusative case used for?"
Students: "Two things: after most prepositions and for the direct object"
Teacher: "Give the prepositions you know that take the accusative case."
Students: "*ad, ante, post, super, apud,* and *per*"
Teacher: "What is a direct object?"
Students: "The word that the subject is doing something to."
Teacher: "Good. What does an -us word look like in the accusative case?"
Students: "-um"
Teacher: "Good. Give five -us words in the accusative."
Students: "*campum, lupum, gladium, nuntium, pullum*"
Teacher: "What does an -er word look like in the accusative case?"
Students: "-um. But the -r stays, and the e usually drops out."
Teacher: "Give five examples."
Students: "*agrum, cultrum, magistrum, ministrum, puerum*"
Teacher: "What does an -um word look like in the accusative case?"
Students: "-um"
Teacher: "How do you tell if an -um word is nominative or accusative then?
Students: "You have to see what the sentence needs. Does it need a subject or a direct object?"

Teacher: "Give five examples of *-um* words in the accusative case."
Students: "*oppidum, aedificium, folium, monstrum, saxum*"
Teacher: "What does an *-a* word look like in the accusative case?"
Students: "*-am*"
Teacher: "Give five examples of *-a* words in the accusative."
Students: "*puellam, feminam, insulam, sellam, mensam*"
Teacher: "Good work!"

Dative Review:

Teacher: "What is the dative case used for?"
Students: "Indirect Object"
Teacher: "What have you learned that an indirect object can do?"
Students: "It tells us to whom something is given."
Teacher: "What in a sentence makes you look for a dative word?"
Students: "The verb *dat*."
Teacher: "What does an *-us* word look like in the dative case?
Students: "*-o*"
Teacher: "What other case ends in *-o*?"
Students: "ablative"
Teacher: "How do you know whether a word is dative or ablative?"
Students: "If there is a preposition before it, then it is probably ablative; if the sentence has *dat*, it is probably dative.
Teacher: "Give five examples of an *-us* word in the dative."
Students: "*fluvio, lupo, nuntio, deo, medico*"
Teacher: "What does an *-er* word look like in the dative?"
Students: "*-o*, but the *-r* stays and the *e* usually drops out."
Teacher: "Give four examples of an *-er* word in the dative."
Students: "*magistro, ministro, puero, viro*"
Teacher: "What does an *-um* word look like in the dative?"
Students: "*-o*"
Teacher: "Give examples of an *-um* word in the dative."
Students: "*monstro, oppido, folio, saxo, aedificio*"
Teacher: "Would you be likely to see *folio* as a dative word?"
Students: "No. Why would you give something to a rock?"
Teacher: "Well, I know I wouldn't, but maybe someone would. What does an *-a* word look like in the dative?"
Students: "*-ae*"
Teacher: "What two other endings does *-ae* look like?"
Students: "genitive, and nominative plural"
Teacher: "How do you know which case it is if they all look the same?"
Students: "You have to see what the sentence needs. If it needs a plural subject, it is probably nominative; if it needs an indirect object, it is probably dative; if it makes sense answering whose, it is probably genitive."
Teacher: "Give five examples of *-a* words in the dative."
Students: "*feminae, puellae, sellae, mensae, insulae*"
Teacher: "Great job!"

Genitive Review:

Teacher: "What is the genitive case used for?"
Students: "possession"
Teacher: "What question does a word in the genitive case usually answer?"
Students: "Whose?"
Teacher: "What is the genitive ending for an -us word?
Students: "-i"
Teacher: "How do you know whether a word is genitive or nominative plural?"
Students: "You have to see what the sentence needs. Does it need a plural subject or a word showing possession?"
Teacher: "Give five examples of -us words in the genitive case."
Students: "*fluvii, campi, lupi, medici, nuntii*"
Teacher: "What is the genitive ending for an -er word?
Students: "-i, but the -r stays and the e usually drops out."
Teacher: "Give five examples of -er words in the genitive case."
Students: "*pueri, viri, magistri, ministri, agri*"
Teacher: "What is the genitive ending of an -um word?"
Students: "-i"
Teacher: "Give five examples of an -um word in the genitive case."
Students: "*monstri, oppidi, aedificii, saxi, folii*"
Teacher: "What is the genitive ending of an -a word?"
Students: "-ae"
Teacher: "Give five examples of -a words in the genitive case."
Students: "*puellae, feminae, mensae, sellae, insulae*"
Teacher: "Very good!"

Lesson 24

Vocabula

- *aranea* - spider
- *ala* - wing
- *sagitta* - arrow
- *porcus* - pig
- *lectus* - bed
- *lilium* - lily
- *signum* - sign

Lesson: Ablative Plural

As the students have probably noticed as they have been filling out their case ending charts, there is a space for the plural version of each case. At this point, your students only know how to use the nominative plural for each type of word (-us words, -er words, -um words, and -a words). Over the next five lessons your students will learn the plural versions of each case, so they will be able to use plural words in all the same contexts that they can singular words.

In this lesson, your students will learn the plural version of the ablative for all the different types of words they have learned: -us words, -er words, -um words, and -a words. The good news is that all of them change to the same ending in the ablative plural: *-is* (pronounced "ees"). So, *puer cum* **lupo** *est* means "the boy is with the **wolf**." But *puer cum* **lupis** *est* means "the boy is with the **wolves**." And, *puer cum* **magistro** *est* means "the boy is with the **teacher**", but "*puer cum* **magistris** *est* means "the boy is with the **teachers**." Likewise, *puer cum* **folio** *est* means "the boy is with the **leaf**", but *puer cum* **foliis** *est* means "the boy is with the **leaves**." And, *puer cum puellā est* means "the boy is with the girl", but *puer cum puellis est* means "the boy is with the girls".

An easy way to drill this is class is to call out any word the students have learned while the students write it on their personal whiteboards in the ablative singular and plural.

Teacher: "*puer*"
Students: (on whiteboards) *puero, pueris*
Teacher: "*monstrum*"
Students: (on whiteboards) *monstro, monstris*
Teacher: "*puella*"
Students: (on whiteboards) *puellā, puellis*
Teacher: "*folium*"
Students: (on whiteboards) *folio, foliis*
Teacher: "*fluvius*"
Students: (on whiteboards) *fluvio, fluviis*

Regulae

- *-Us* words, *-er* words, *-um* words, and *-a* words have the ending *-is* in the ablative plural.

Tabulae (Traditional Order)

US

CASE	FUNCTION	SG.	PL.
Normal		US	I
Genitive	Possession	I	
Dative	Indirect Object	O	
Accusative	After prepositions *ad, ante, post, super, and apud* As a direct object	UM	
Ablative	After prepositions *in, cum, ab, ex,* and *sub*	O	**IS**

Tabulae (British Order)

US

CASE	FUNCTION	SG.	PL.
Nominative	Subject	US	I
Accusative	After prepositions *ad, ante, post, super, and apud* & As a direct object	UM	
Genitive	Possession	I	
Dative	Indirect Object	O	
Ablative	After prepositions *in, cum, ab, ex,* and *sub*	O	**IS**

Tabulae (Traditional Order)

ER

CASE	FUNCTION	SG.	PL.
Nominative	Subject	ER	I
Genitive	Possession	I	
Dative	Indirect Object	O	
Accusative	After prepositions *ad*, *ante*, *post*, *super*, and *apud* & As a direct object	UM	
Ablative	After prepositions *in*, *cum*, *ab*, *ex*, and *sub*	O	**IS**

Tabulae (British Order)

ER

CASE	FUNCTION	SG.	PL.
Nominative	Subject	ER	I
Accusative	After prepositions *ad*, *ante*, *post*, *super*, and *apud* & As a direct object	UM	
Genitive	Possession	I	
Dative	Indirect Object	O	
Ablative	After prepositions *in*, *cum*, *ab*, *ex*, and *sub*	O	**IS**

Tabulae (Traditional Order)

UM

CASE	FUNCTION	SG.	PL.
Nominative	Subject	UM	A
Genitive	Possession	I	
Dative	Indirect Object	O	
Accusative	After prepositions *ad, ante, post, super, and apud* & As a direct object	UM	
Ablative	After prepositions *in, cum, ab, ex*, and *sub*	O	**IS**

Tabulae (British Order)

UM

CASE	FUNCTION	SG.	PL.
Nominative	Subject	UM	A
Accusative	After prepositions *ad, ante, post, super, and apud* & As a direct object	UM	
Genitive	Possession	I	
Dative	Indirect Object	O	
Ablative	After prepositions *in, cum, ab, ex*, and *sub*	O	**IS**

Tabulae (Traditional Order)

A

CASE	FUNCTION	SG.	PL.
Nominative	Subject	A	AE
Genitive	Possession	AE	
Dative	Indirect Object	AE	
Accusative	Direct Object After prepositions *ad, ante, post, super, apud*, and *per*	AM	
Ablative	After prepositions *in, cum, ab, ex, sub, de*	Ā	**IS**

Tabulae (British Order)

A

CASE	FUNCTION	SG.	PL.
Nominative	Subject	A	AE
Accusative	Direct Object After prepositions *ad, ante, post, super, apud*, and *per*	AM	
Genitive	Possession	AE	
Dative	Indirect Object	AE	
Ablative	After prepositions *in, cum, ab, ex, sub, de*	Ā	**IS**

Lesson 25

Vocabula

- *taberna* - store; a Roman store was often just a booth set up in the city square
- *tabernarius* - store keeper; this man was usually not the owner, and often a slave
- *silva* - forest
- *mendum* - mistake; this is specifically a mistake in writing--not a mistake in general
- *gallus* - rooster
- *regula* - ruler; a tool for drawing a straight line
- *horologium* - clock; a Roman "clock" was a sundial or hourglass

- *septem* - seven
- *octo* - eight

Lesson: Accusative Plural

In this lesson your students will learn the plural endings for the accusative case. This is more challenging than learning the ablative plural, because each type of word gets its own ending. *-Us* and *-er* words change to *-os*, *-um* words change to *-a*, and *-a* words change to *-as*. There are a few things that you can point out to your students to make this easier. First, point out that *-o* has shown up in *-us* words before. The accusative plural ending *-os* just adds an *s* to this *o*.

Teacher: "The new ending for *-us* words is *-os*. Have you all seen the letter *o* in any forms of *-us* words before?"
Students: "Yes, in the ablative and the dative cases."
Teacher: "That's right. *-Us* words actually have the letter *o* in them often."

Second, point out that *a* has shown up in *-a* words before. The accusative plural ending *-as* just adds an *s* to this *a* in a similar way.

Teacher: "The new ending for *-a* words is *-as*. Have you all seen the letter *a* in any forms of *-a* words before?"
Students: "Um...all over the place. There is an *a* in almost every form."
Teacher: "That's right. *-A* words are called *-a* words for a reason. The accusative plural just adds an *s* to that *a*."

Third, point out that *-um* words are the ones that truly act differently. There is a rule that *-um* words always look the same in the nominative and the accusative.

Teacher: "The new ending for *-um* words is *a*. I know that seems very unusual, but have you seen that ending *-a* in an *-um* word before?"
Students: "It is in the nominative plural."
Teacher: "Right. So what is the nominative plural ending for *-um* words?"
Students: "*a*"
Teacher: "What is the accusative plural ending for *-um* words?"
Students: "*a*"
Teacher: "What is the nominative singular ending for *-um* words?"
Students: "*um*"
Teacher: "What is the accusative singular ending for *-um* words?"

Students: *"um"*
Teacher: "Anyone see a pattern?"
Students: "The nominative and accusative are the same."
Teacher: "Yes, in *-um* words the nominative and accusative are always the same. In fact, it is a rule."

Like with the ablative case, an easy way to drill this is class is to call out any word the students have learned while the students write it on their personal whiteboards in the accusative singular and plural.

Teacher: *"puer"*
Students: (on whiteboards) *puerum, pueros*
Teacher: *"monstrum"*
Students: (on whiteboards) *monstrum, monstra*
Teacher: *"puella"*
Students: (on whiteboards) *puellam, puellas*
Teacher: *"folium"*
Students: (on whiteboards) *folium, folia*
Teacher: *"fluvius"*
Students: (on whiteboards) *fluvium, fluvios*

Regulae

- *-Us* and *-er* words in the accusative, plural get the ending *-os*.
- *-Um* words in the accusative, plural get the ending *-a*.
- *-A* words in the accusative, plural get the ending *-as*.

Tabulae (Traditional Order)

US

CASE	FUNCTION	SG.	PL.
Nominative	Subject	US	I
Genitive	Possession	I	
Dative	Indirect Object	O	
Accusative	After prepositions *ad, ante, post, super, and apud* & As a direct object	UM	**OS**
Ablative	After prepositions *in, cum, ab, ex,* and *sub*	O	IS

Tabulae (British Order)

US

CASE	FUNCTION	SG.	PL.
Nominative	Subject	US	I
Accusative	After prepositions *ad, ante, post, super, and apud* & As a direct object	UM	**OS**
Genitive	Possession	I	
Dative	Indirect Object	O	
Ablative	After prepositions *in, cum, ab, ex,* and *sub*	O	IS

Tabulae (Traditional Order)

ER

CASE	FUNCTION	SG.	PL.
Nominative	Subject	ER	I
Genitive	Possession	I	
Dative	Indirect Object	O	
Accusative	After prepositions *ad, ante, post, super, and apud* & As a direct object	UM	**OS**
Ablative	After prepositions *in, cum, ab, ex*, and *sub*	O	IS

Tabulae (British Order)

ER

CASE	FUNCTION	SG.	PL.
Nominative	Subject	ER	I
Accusative	After prepositions *ad, ante, post, super, and apud* & As a direct object	UM	**OS**
Genitive	Possession	I	
Dative	Indirect Object	O	
Ablative	After prepositions *in, cum, ab, ex*, and *sub*	O	IS

Tabulae (Traditional Order)

UM

CASE	FUNCTION	SG.	PL.
Nominative	Subject	UM	A
Genitive	Possession	I	
Dative	Indirect Object	O	
Accusative	After prepositions *ad, ante, post, super, and apud* & As a direct object	UM	**A**
Ablative	After prepositions *in, cum, ab, ex,* and *sub*	O	IS

Tabulae (British Order)

UM

CASE	FUNCTION	SG.	PL.
Nominative	Subject	UM	A
Accusative	After prepositions *ad, ante, post, super, and apud* & As a direct object	UM	**A**
Genitive	Possession	I	
Dative	Indirect Object	O	
Ablative	After prepositions *in, cum, ab, ex,* and *sub*	O	IS

Tabulae (Traditional Order)

A

CASE	FUNCTION	SG.	PL.
Nominative	Subject	A	AE
Genitive	Possession	AE	
Dative	Indirect Object	AE	
Accusative	Direct Object After prepositions *ad, ante, post, super, apud,* and *per*	AM	**AS**
Ablative	After prepositions *in, cum, ab, ex, sub, de*	Ā	IS

Tabulae (British Order)

A

CASE	FUNCTION	SG.	PL.
Nominative	Subject	A	AE
Accusative	Direct Object After prepositions *ad, ante, post, super, apud,* and *per*	AM	**AS**
Genitive	Possession	AE	
Dative	Indirect Object	AE	
Ablative	After prepositions *in, cum, ab, ex, sub, de*	Ā	IS

Lesson 26

Vocabula

- *vocat* - calls
- *audit* - hears
- *iubet* - commands
- *monstrat* - shows; this is specifically to show by pointing out with a finger
- *dicit* - says; this word can also mean "speak" or "speak about"
- *petit* - goes after
- *vult* - wants

In this lesson your students will learn the verb *dicit* which normally means "says", but in this course will mean "speaks or talks about". In these scenes, the boy has a speech bubble, and in the speech bubble is the thing he is talking about. If there is a girl in the speech bubble, the boy is talking about a girl.

Lesson: Accusative Plural as Direct Object

In this lesson your students will see the accusative plural used as a direct object. Since the students used the accusative plural in the last lesson with prepositions, there are no new forms to learn. This should give your students a little more time to master these accusative plural endings.

A good additional drill to help solidify the forms is to have your students do transformations from singular to plural and plural to singular every once in a while when the class is working on an example.

Example: *Puer puellas monstrat.*
Teacher: "Okay, now that we have done this sentence, let's change the direct object to the singular. Suppose there were only one girl he was pointing at: what would that form have to be?"
Students: "*puellam*"
Teacher: "Exactly!"

Lesson 27

Vocabula

- *anima* - spirit; this word also means "breath"
- *stella* - star
- *amica* - friend (girl); this word can mean friend that is a girl or girlfriend
- *culina* - kitchen
- *cocus* - cook
- *fumus* - smoke
- *sepulcrum* - grave

- *magicus* - magic; this word is an adjective; its ending changes to *magicum* in the story, but no need to explain why yet

Lesson: Dative Plural

In this lesson your students will learn to use the plural form of the dative and will once again practice a number of sentences with indirect objects. Since the indirect object is a difficult concept, never pass up the opportunity to review with the students the difference: a direct object is what the subject is doing something to; the indirect object often answers to whom something is being given. The dative plural ending is -is ("ees") for -us words, -er words, -um words, and -a words. In other words, the dative plural looks exactly like the ablative plural.

Even though the dative plural is the new concept for this lesson, it will probably not be the most difficult aspect of this lesson, since all the words take the same "is" ending. The more difficult part of this lesson will likely be what your students have been working on these past two weeks: the accusative plural endings. Do not be discouraged if your students continue to struggle with these endings--they are difficult and require time and practice to master. It is important to let them know that *everybody* struggles with these forms and that it is completely normal to miss them frequently. In fact, this is probably the most difficult thing they will learn in Latin during this course. When students get these endings wrong, ask them to refer to the *Tabulae* section of their student workbook to correct the mistake. The repetition of missing an ending, being called out on it, needing to look at a chart, and correcting it is very, very effective--the teacher just needs to be both relentless and encouraging.

Example: *Puer magistris gladium dat.*
Teacher: "There are a lot of words here, so let's be careful to see what each one is doing. Which word here is the subject?"
Students: "*Puer!*"
Teacher: "Good. How did you know?"
Students: "It is in the nominative case."
Teacher: "Good. What is the verb of the sentence?"
Students: "*dat.*"
Teacher: "Good! What two things does *dat* usually need in a sentence?"
Students: "A direct object and an indirect object."
Teacher: "Where is the direct object, and how do you know?"
Students: "*Gladium*. It is in the accusative case."
Teacher: "Where is the indirect object, and how do you know?"
Students: "*Magistris*. It is in the dative plural."

Again, if you have extra time to do some transformations as a class, it can really be worth it. Changing a single word or multiple ones from singular to plural or plural to singular is very helpful.

Regulae

- *-Us* words, *-er* words, *-um* words, and *-a* words in the dative, plural have the ending *-is*.

Tabulae (Traditional Order)

US

CASE	FUNCTION	SG.	PL.
Nominative	Subject	US	I
Genitive	Possession	I	
Dative	Indirect Object	O	**IS**
Accusative	After prepositions *ad, ante, post, super,* and *apud* & As a direct object	UM	OS
Ablative	After prepositions *in, cum, ab, ex,* and *sub*	O	IS

Tabulae (British Order)

US

CASE	FUNCTION	SG.	PL.
Nominative	Subject	US	I
Accusative	After prepositions *ad, ante, post, super,* and *apud* & As a direct object	UM	OS
Genitive	Possession	I	
Dative	Indirect Object	O	**IS**
Ablative	After prepositions *in, cum, ab, ex,* and *sub*	O	IS

Tabulae (Traditional Order)

ER

CASE	FUNCTION	SG.	PL.
Nominative	Subject	ER	I
Genitive	Possession	I	
Dative	Indirect Object	O	**IS**
Accusative	After prepositions *ad, ante, post, super, and apud* & As a direct object	UM	OS
Ablative	After prepositions *in, cum, ab, ex,* and *sub*	O	IS

Tabulae (British Order)

ER

CASE	FUNCTION	SG.	PL.
Nominative	Subject	ER	I
Accusative	After prepositions *ad, ante, post, super, and apud* & As a direct object	UM	OS
Genitive	Possession	I	
Dative	Indirect Object	O	**IS**
Ablative	After prepositions *in, cum, ab, ex,* and *sub*	O	IS

Tabulae (Traditional Order)

UM

CASE	FUNCTION	SG.	PL.
Nominative	Subject	UM	A
Genitive	Possession	I	
Dative	Indirect Object	O	**IS**
Accusative	After prepositions *ad, ante, post, super, and apud* & As a direct object	UM	A
Ablative	After prepositions *in, cum, ab, ex,* and *sub*	O	IS

Tabulae (British Order)

UM

CASE	FUNCTION	SG.	PL.
Nominative	Subject	UM	A
Accusative	After prepositions *ad, ante, post, super, and apud* & As a direct object	UM	A
Genitive	Possession	I	
Dative	Indirect Object	O	**IS**
Ablative	After prepositions *in, cum, ab, ex,* and *sub*	O	IS

Tabulae (Traditional Order)

A

CASE	FUNCTION	SG.	PL.
Nominative	Subject	A	AE
Genitive	Possession	AE	
Dative	Indirect Object	AE	**IS**
Accusative	Direct Object After prepositions *ad, ante, post, super, apud,* and *per*	AM	AS
Ablative	After prepositions *in, cum, ab, ex, sub, de*	Ā	IS

Tabulae (British Order)

A

CASE	FUNCTION	SG.	PL.
Nominative	Subject	A	AE
Accusative	Direct Object After prepositions *ad, ante, post, super, apud,* and *per*	AM	AS
Genitive	Possession	AE	
Dative	Indirect Object	AE	**IS**
Ablative	After prepositions *in, cum, ab, ex, sub, de*	Ā	IS

Lesson 28

Vocabula

- *instrumentum* - tool
- *lacrima* - tear
- *gemma* - jewel
- *margarita* - pearl
- *linea* - string
- *pretium* - price
- *titulus* - title

- *novem* - nine
- *decem* - ten

Lesson: Genitive Plural

In this lesson your students will learn the genitive plural endings for *-us, -er, -um,* and *-a* words. These are the last noun endings they will learn this year. As they have learned before, the genitive case often shows possession, like *-'s* in English. But sometimes a thing is "possessed" by more than one thing. In such cases, it is necessary to use a noun that is both genitive and plural. In English, this is sometimes accomplished with *-s'*; however, this is confusing even to English speakers and probably not helpful to bring up with your students.

In Latin, an *-us, -er,* or *-um* word takes the ending *-orum* (oh-rum) in the genitive plural. So, *pecunia servorum* would mean, "the money **of the servants**"; *lacrimae puerorum* would mean, "the tears **of the boys**"; *pulli monstrorum* means "the chicks **of the monsters**".

An *-a* word in the genitive plural takes a similar ending: *-arum* (ah-rum). Make sure to point out to your students that the ending is the same, but with an *a* instead of an *o*.

Genitive plural endings are easy to recognize because they are four letters long and do not look like any other endings. However, sometimes students will only see the last two letters (*um*) and confuse it with the accusative case. If a student makes this mistake, instruct him to pronounce every syllable in the word aloud. It is much easier to overlook

Like with the other cases, an easy way to drill this is class is to call out any word the students have learned while the students write it on their personal whiteboards in the accusative singular and plural.

Teacher: "*puer*"
Students: (on whiteboards) *pueri, puerorum*
Teacher: "*monstrum*"
Students: (on whiteboards) *monstri, monstrorum*
Teacher: "*puella*"
Students: (on whiteboards) *puellae, puellarum*
Teacher: "*folium*"
Students: (on whiteboards) *folii, foliorum*
Teacher: "*fluvius*"
Students: (on whiteboards) *fluvii, fluviorum*

Regulae:

- *-Us* words, *-er* words, and *-um* words in the genitive plural have the ending *-orum*.
- *-A* words in the genitive plural have the ending *-arum*.

Tabulae (Traditional Order)

US

CASE	FUNCTION	SG.	PL.
Nominative	Subject	US	I
Genitive	Possession	I	**ORUM**
Dative	Indirect Object	O	IS
Accusative	After prepositions *ad*, *ante*, *post*, *super*, and *apud* & As a direct object	UM	OS
Ablative	After prepositions *in*, *cum*, *ab*, *ex*, and *sub*	O	IS

Tabulae (British Order)

US

CASE	FUNCTION	SG.	PL.
Nominative	Subject	US	I
Accusative	After prepositions *ad*, *ante*, *post*, *super*, and *apud* & As a direct object	UM	OS
Genitive	Possession	I	**ORUM**
Dative	Indirect Object	O	IS
Ablative	After prepositions *in*, *cum*, *ab*, *ex*, and *sub*	O	IS

Tabulae (Traditional Order)

ER

CASE	FUNCTION	SG.	PL.
Nominative	Subject	ER	I
Genitive	Possession	I	**ORUM**
Dative	Indirect Object	O	IS
Accusative	After prepositions *ad, ante, post, super, and apud* & As a direct object	UM	OS
Ablative	After prepositions *in, cum, ab, ex,* and *sub*	O	IS

Tabulae (British Order)

ER

CASE	FUNCTION	SG.	PL.
Nominative	Subject	ER	I
Accusative	After prepositions *ad, ante, post, super, and apud* & As a direct object	UM	OS
Genitive	Possession	I	**ORUM**
Dative	Indirect Object	O	IS
Ablative	After prepositions *in, cum, ab, ex,* and *sub*	O	IS

Tabulae (Traditional Order)

UM

CASE	FUNCTION	SG.	PL.
Nominative	Subject	UM	A
Genitive	Possession	I	**ORUM**
Dative	Indirect Object	O	IS
Accusative	After prepositions *ad, ante, post, super, and apud* & As a direct object	UM	A
Ablative	After prepositions *in, cum, ab, ex,* and *sub*	O	IS

Tabulae (British Order)

UM

CASE	FUNCTION	SG.	PL.
Nominative	Subject	UM	A
Accusative	After prepositions *ad, ante, post, super, and apud* & As a direct object	UM	A
Genitive	Possession	I	**ORUM**
Dative	Indirect Object	O	IS
Ablative	After prepositions *in, cum, ab, ex,* and *sub*	O	IS

Tabulae (Traditional Order)

A

CASE	FUNCTION	SG.	PL.
Nominative	Subject	A	AE
Genitive	Possession	AE	**ARUM**
Dative	Indirect Object	AE	IS
Accusative	Direct Object After prepositions *ad*, *ante*, *post*, *super*, *apud*, and *per*	AM	AS
Ablative	After prepositions *in*, *cum*, *ab*, *ex*, *sub*, *de*	Ā	IS

Tabulae (British Order)

A

CASE	FUNCTION	SG.	PL.
Nominative	Subject	A	AE
Accusative	Direct Object After prepositions *ad*, *ante*, *post*, *super*, *apud*, and *per*	AM	AS
Genitive	Possession	AE	**ARUM**
Dative	Indirect Object	AE	IS
Ablative	After prepositions *in*, *cum*, *ab*, *ex*, *sub*, *de*	Ā	IS

Lesson 29

Vocabula

- *aperit* - opens
- *claudit* - closes
- *emit* - buys
- *vendit* - sells
- *ascendit* - climbs up
- *descendit* - goes down
- *cadit* - falls

Charts

Traditionally, students have used case charts and case chants to help memorize the case endings. These can be valuable tools, especially if their limits are understood clearly. Once children understand how the endings work and what they mean, charts can be used to the greatest effect by *organizing* what they already know. Now that your students know what the five major cases are and how they are used, charts are particularly useful for helping your students keep the endings distinct in their minds. One way to do this is by having students fill out empty charts on their own. After your students fill out charts, quiz the students on the meaning of the chart they filled out. For example:

Teacher: "You wrote the word 'nominative' here. What does that mean?"
Students: "It is the name of a case."
Teacher: "What is a case?"
Students: "It is an ending that shows you what a word is doing in the sentence."
Teacher: "What does the nominative case do?"
Students: "It shows the subject, just like I wrote on the chart."
Teacher: "What does this *-us* mean here?"
Students: "This chart is for words that end in *-us* like *lupus*."
Teacher: "What does the *-i* mean here?"
Students: "That is the plural."
Teacher: "The plural of what?"
Students: "The plural of the nominative case?"

This kind of question and answer will help your students review all the old rules and definitions they learned over the year and make sure that the chart is meaningful to them. Remember that 3rd-graders do not always think in charts naturally--they may need help linking it to its meaning.

Filling out charts is not only good practice, but it is also a great way to assess the student's progress for the year. Consider having your students fill out a chart for each of the types of words they learned this year as an end-of-the-year exam. If you have enough time to sit down with each student alone, quiz each one orally about the meaning of the different parts of the chart. Frequently, you will find that a student that has made mistakes in filling out a chart understands much more than he represents on paper--a few questions can tease out the right answers.

Chants

Many teachers like to have their students chant endings (for *-us*, *-um*, and *-a* words) in a linear fashion, much in the same way that younger students chant the letters of the English alphabet. (This is typically done in the traditional order--not the British.) For example:

Teacher: "Chant the endings for an *-us* noun."
Students: "*us, i, o,* um, *o, i, orum, is, os, is*"
Teacher: "Chant the endings for an *-um* noun."
Students: "*um, i, o,* um, *o, a, orum, is, a, is*"
Teacher: "Chant the endings for an *-a* noun."
Students: "*a, ae, ae, am, ā, ae, arum, is, as, is*"

Chanting is easy (and fun) for a class to do as a whole; however, it does not teach students what endings mean, and even what they are associated with. To use chants to their greatest effect, mix them with filling out charts (as described above). Also, try alternating chants with singular-plural chants for individual cases, as follows:

Example: *lupus*
Teacher: "Accusative!"
Students: "*lupum, lupos*"
Teacher: "Ablative!"
Students: "*lupo, lupis*"
Teacher: "Nominative!"
Students: "*lupus, lupi*"
Teacher: "Genitive!"
Students: "*lupi, luporum*"

If students have trouble with these singular-plural chants at first, draw a chart up on the board so they can see it while they chant. After the first round, start erasing endings here and there. Eventually, work up to the point where the students do not need the chart at all. If you have time, work through a new word every day. After a few weeks of reviewing this way, students should have their endings down much more firmly.

Lesson: Plural Verbs

So far, your students have only used one plural verb: *sunt*. In this lesson your students will finally learn how to make other verbs plural. The following information is good for the teacher to understand, but is not necessary to teach to elementary students. They will learn a simplified version of this. Most Latin verbs fall into four or five categories that are called conjugations: 1st, 2nd, 3rd, 3rd (-io), and 4th. Verbs that have an *a* right before the ending are in the 1st conjugation, such as *ambula-t, pulsa-t,* and *voca-t*. (Note that the dash is added here to divide the verb stem from its ending.) In this course, we call these verbs "*-a* verbs" because children usually find the descriptive term much easier to remember than 1st conjugation. Verbs that have an *e* right before the ending are in the 2nd conjugation, such as *vide-t, ride-t,* and *time-t*. This course calls these "*-e* verbs". Verbs that have a consonant right before the ending are in the 3rd declension, such as *sum-it, pon-it,* and *claud-it*. (Note that the *i* in the ending *-it* is now part of the ending.) Verbs that end in a weak *i* are in the 3rd -io conjugation, such as *cap(i)-t,* and *iac(i)-t*. Weak just means that the *i* in the verb drops out of some forms, and this is not important in this course. In this course, we will show these with an *i* in parentheses: *(i)*. Finally, verbs that end in a strong *i* are in the fourth declension, such as *dormi-t* and *audi-t*. We call these *-i* verbs.

All this can be very confusing, so it is much better to simplify this for the students as follows. There are three kinds of verbs your students need to recognize: *-a* verbs, *-e* verbs, and other kinds of verbs. An *-a* or *-e* verb will take the ending *-nt* when it is plural. For example, *ambula-nt, pulsa-nt, voca-nt, vide-nt, ride-nt,* and *time-nt* are all plural versions of the verbs. However, any other kind of verb will take the ending *-unt* when it is plural. For example, *sum-unt, pon-unt, claud-unt, cap(i)-unt, iac(i)-unt, dormi-unt,* and *audi-unt*. In the exercises, we will always provide the verb stem, so students just need to remember to add either *-nt* or *-unt*. By the time students are writing out their sentences, they will likely remember it by sound. That said, when students are writing in their student workbooks or doing quizzes, it may be necessary to write the verb stems on the board for the students. Or, the teacher may offer to help students with the verb stems if they need help. This is completely fine. At this point, the students just need to know that the ending is -nt after *a* and *e*, but *-unt* in other verbs.

Regulae

- A-verbs and e-verbs add the ending *-nt* in the plural.
- Other verbs add the ending *-unt* in the plural.

Lesson 30

There is no new vocabulary or grammar introduced in lesson 30. By this point, your students know how to use all five cases for *-us* words, *-er* words, *-um* words, and *-a* words. They also know how to use verbs in the singular and plural. This is only a small part of Latin grammar, but it is a very, very important one. If students understand the concepts of the cases and can use them with simple words like these, they will have a firm foundation to build on moving forward. Additionally, with these forms your students will now know enough to read some simple stories in Latin. Reading stories in Latin will help your students both enjoy what they have learned and help them remember it. If you have the time before the end of the year, consider spending some of it reading simple Latin. There are a number of simple Latin novellas available on the market, but we particularly recommend the first five chapters of the most successful Latin Reader of our time, *Lingua Latina Per Se Illustrata Pars I: Familia Romana*. There are also some additional stories and dialogues that go with these chapters in *Colloquia Personarum* and *Fabellae Latinae*. Your students will know most of the vocabulary and all of the grammar for these chapters already.

Workbook Answer Key

Lesson 1a

1. oculi
2. digiti
3. stili
4. fluvii
5. campi
6. Puer in fluvio est.
7. Puer in campo est.
8. Puer in horto est.
9. Puer in digito est.
10. Puer in stilo est.

Is *stilus* singular or plural? singular
Is *campi* singular or plural? plural
Is *fluvius* singular or plural? singular
Is *digiti* singular or plural? plural

Lesson 1b

1. digiti
2. stili
3. fluvii
4. campi
5. horti
6. Puer in horto est.
7. Puer in fluvio est.
8. Puer in digito est.
9. Puer in stilo est.
10. Puer in oculo est.

6: Ubi est puer? in horto
7: Ubi est puer? in fluvio
Is *oculus* normal or ablative? normal
Is *campo* normal or ablative? ablative

Lesson 2a

1. Puer cum servo est.
2. Puer cum domino est.
3. Puer cum lupo est.
4. servi
5. lupi
6. Puer ab lupo ambulat.
7. Puer ab fluvio ambulat.
8. Puer ab muro ambulat.
9. Puer ab horto ambulat.
10. Puer ab campo ambulat.

Give three Latin prepositions. in, cum, ab
3: Ubi est puer? cum lupo
Is *murus* singular or plural? singular
Is *fluvius* normal or ablative? normal

Lesson 2b

1. Puer cum lupo est.
2. Puer cum domino est.
3. lupi
4. fluvii
5. oculi
6. Puer in fluvio est.
7. Puer in mundo est.
8. Puer ab lupo ambulat.
9. Puer ab horto ambulat.
10. Puer ab mundo ambulat.

1: Ubi est puer? cum lupo
6: Ubi est puer? in fluvio
Is *muri* singular or plural? plural
Is *muro* normal or ablative? ablative

93

Lesson 3a

1. Lupus sub petaso est.
2. Lupus sub equo est..
3. Puer sub gladio est.
4. Puer sub fluvio est.
5. Lupus ex horto ambulat.
6. Lupus ex fluvio ambulat.
7. Lupus ex campo ambulat.
8. Puer ex digito ambulat.
9. calcei
10. Lupus ab horto ambulat.

Give five Latin prepositions. in, cum, ab, ex, sub
2: Ubi est lupus? sub equo
Is *calceus* singular or plural? singular
Is *horto* normal or ablative? ablative

Lesson 3b

1. Lupus sub calceo est.
2. Lupus ex campo ambulat.
3. Lupus ex fluvio ambulat.
4. Lupus ex horto ambulat.
5. Anulus in digito est.
6. Puer cum servo est.
7. Puer cum lupo est.
8. Puer ab muro ambulat.
9. Puer ab cibo ambulat.
10. Puer ex horto ambulat.

5: Ubi est anulus? in digito
7: Ubi est puer? cum lupo
8: Is *muro* normal or ablative? ablative
5: Is *anulus* normal or ablative? normal

Lesson 4a

1. Puer in campo dormit.
2. Puer in equo dormit.
3. Puer in equo sedet.
4. Puer in campo sedet.
5. Puer in fluvio cogitat.
6. Puer sub cibo cogitat.
7. Lupus sub calceo est.
8. petasi
9. calcei
10. anuli

1: Ubi puer dormit? in campo
3: Ubi puer sedet? in equo
5: Ubi puer cogitat? in fluvio
Is *petasi* singular or plural? plural

Lesson 4b

1. Puer in horto legit.
2. Puer in campo legit.
3. Puer in campo scribit.
4. Puer in horto scribit.
5. Puer sub gladio stat.
6. Puer in campo stat.
7. Puer ab muro ambulat.
8. Puer ab lupo ambulat.
9. Puer sub fluvio est.
10. Lupus sub petaso est.

1: Ubi puer legit? in horto
3: Ubi puer scribit? in campo
5: Ubi puer stat? sub gladio
Is *petaso* normal or ablative? ablative

Lesson 5a

1. Puer ad hortum ambulat.
2. Puer ad cavum ambulat.
3. Puer ad equum ambulat.
4. Puer ab horto ambulat.
5. Puer ab cavo ambulat.
6. Puer ab equo ambulat.
7. Puer ante hortum est.
8. Puer ante mundum est.
9. Digitus in naso est.
10. nasi

1: Is *hortum* ablative or accusative? accusative
5: Is *cavo* ablative or accusative? ablative
8: Is *mundum* ablative or accusative? accusative
9: Is *naso* ablative or accusative? ablative

Lesson 5b

1. Puer ad fluvium ambulat.
2. Puer ab fluvio ambulat.
3. Puer ad hortum ambulat.
4. Lupus ab horto ambulat.
5. Lupus ad capillum ambulat.
6. Lupus ab filio ambulat.
7. Puer ante hortum est.
8. Puer in muro est.
9. mundi
10. Puer sub gladio sedet.

1: Is *fluvium* ablative or accusative? accusative
2: Is fluvio ablative or accusative? ablative
What prepositions take ablative? in, cum, ab, ex, sub
What prepositions take accusative? ad, ante, post, super, apud

Lesson 6a

1. Lupus post campum est.
2. Lupus super hortum est.
3. Lupus post cibum est.
4. Asinus ante saccum est.
5. Puer ad fluvium ambulat.
6. Puer in horto est.
7. Puer in equo sedet.
8. Ursus post saccum est.
9. Asinus in fluvio est.
10. Lupus super fluvium est.

1: Ubi est lupus? post campum
4: Ubi est asinus? ante saccum
7: Ubi puer sedet? in equo
What prepositions take accusative? ad, ante, post, super, apud

Lesson 6b

1. Lupus post nasum est
2. Lupus super cavum est
3. Puer apud saccum est
4. Puer ad cavum ambulat
5. Puer ad equum ambulat
6. Puer ab lupo ambulat
7. Lupus ex horto ambulat
8. Asinus in fluvio est
9. Digitus in naso est
10. asini

1: Ubi est lupus? post nasum
4: Is *cavum* ablative or accusative? accusative
8: Quis in fluvio est? in fluvio ?
What prepositions take ablative? in, cum, ab, ex, sub

Lesson 7a

1. Puer murum pulsat.
2. Puer dominum pulsat.
3. Puer equum pulsat.
4. Puer lupum videt.
5. Dominus hortum videt.
6. Puer cibum habet.
7. Puer anulum habet.
8. Puer calceum habet.
9. Dominus cibum habet.
10. Dominus lupum videt.

2: Which word is the direct object? dominum
3: What case is *cibum*? accusative
7: Which word is the direct object? anulum
8: What case is *calceum*? accusative

Lesson 7b

1. Puer murum pulsat.
2. Puer nasum pulsat.
3. Puer anulum habet.
4. Puer calceum habet.
5. Puer petasum habet.
6. Dominus lupum videt.
7. nummi
8. ursi
9. Lupus sub equo est.
10. Lupus ambulat ex horto.

6: What case is *lupum*? accusative
7: Is *nummi* singular or plural? plural
9: Ubi est lupus? sub equo
10: What case is *horto*? ablative

Lesson 8a

1. Puer lupo cibum dat.
2. Puer servo cibum dat.
3. Puer domino cibum dat.
4. Puer equo cibum dat.
5. Puer mundo cibum dat.
6. Dominus lupo nummum dat.
7. Dominus servo calceum dat.
8. Dominus filio calceum dat.
9. Dominus equo calceum dat.
10. Dominus domino calceum dat.

1: What case is *lupo*? dative
1: What case is *cibum*? accusative
6: Which word is the direct object? nummum
6: Which word is the indirect object? lupo

Lesson 8b

1. Puer fluvio cibum dat.
2. Dominus lupo calceum dat.
3. Dominus fluvio calceum dat.
4. Dominus lupo nummum dat.
5. Dominus servo nummum dat.
6. Dominus equo nummum dat.
7. Puer servo gladium dat.
8. Puer in horto legit.
9. Puer sub gladio stat.
10. Puer in campo stat.

1: What case is *fluvio*? dative
4: What case is *nummum*? accusative
8: What case is *horto*? ablative
9: Ubi stat puer? sub gladio

Lesson 9a

1. gladius domini
2. stilus domini
3. equus domini
4. cibus domini
5. gladius servi
6. stilus servi
7. equus servi
8. cibus servi
9. dominus servi
10. anulus servi

2: What case is *domini*? genitive
4: Is *equus* genitive or normal? genitive
What two cases could *fluvio* be? ablative or dative
What case would *gladium* be? accusative

Lesson 9b

1. hortus domini
2. calceus servi
3. cibus lupi
4. stilus lupi
5. Gladius in campo est.
6. Puer sub fluvio est.
7. Puer ad fluvium ambulat.
8. Puer apud fluvium est.
9. Puer servum videt.
10. Puer cibum videt.

1: What case is *domini*? genitive
6: Ubi est puer? sub fluvio
7: Quis ad fluvium ambulat? puer
8: Ubi est puer? apud fluvium

Lesson 10a

1. Lupus ab puero ambulat.
2. Lupus ad puerum ambulat.
3. Dominus puerum videt.
4. Puer viro clipeum dat.
5. Dominus viro calceum dat.
6. Dominus puero clipeum dat.
7. pugnus pueri
8. pullus pueri
9. pueri
10. viri

1: What case is *lupus*? nominative
5: What case is *viro*? dative
6: What case is *clipeum*? accusative
8: What case is *pueri*? genitive

Lesson 10b

1. Lupus ab puero ambulat.
2. Lupus ad puerum ambulat.
3. Lupus ad virum ambulat.
4. Dominus virum videt.
5. Puer viro cibum dat.
6. Puer virum pulsat.
7. pugnus pueri
8. pullus pueri
9. viri
10. Gladius in clipeo est.

4: Quis virum videt? dominus
5: What case is *viro*? dative
6: What case is *virum*? accusative
7: What case is *pueri*? genitive

Lesson 11a

1. Colonus in agro est.
2. Lupus post cultrum est.
3. Lupus ab cultro ambulat.
4. Puer ministrum pulsat.
5. Discipulus magistro librum dat.
6. Puer ministro cultrum dat.
7. liber magistri.
8. culter ministri.
9. pugnus pueri.
10. libri

1: What case is *colonus*? nominative
2: Ubi est lupus? post cultrum
6: What case is *ministro*? ministro
9: What case is *pugnus*? nominative

Lesson 11b

1. Colonus in libro est.
2. Minister in cultro est.
3. liber magistri
4. pugnus pueri
5. cultri
6. Puer ante murum est.
7. Magister ante ludum est.
8. Lupus ex horto ambulat.
9. Lupus ex agro ambulat.
10. Puer cibum habet.

1: Ubi est colonus? in libro
2: What case is *cultro*? ablative
3: What case is *magistri*? genitive
5: What case is *cultri*? nominative (plural)

Lesson 12a

1. Baculum in aedificio est.
2. Tyrannus in oppido est.
3. Puer in saxo est.
4. Magister in tergo est.
5. Puer sub saxo stat.
6. Oppidum sub saxo est.
7. Aedificium sub saxo est.
8. Colonus in agro est.
9. Lupus post librum est.
10. culter ministri

1: What case is *aedificio*? ablative
1: What case is *baculum*? nominative
6: Ubi est oppidum? sub saxo
10: What case is *ministri*? genitive

Lesson 12b

1. Minister in aedificio est.
2. Equus in oppido est.
3. Magister in bracchio est.
4. Discipulus ab saxo ambulat.
5. Puer sub saxo stat.
6. Oppidum sub saxo est.
7. Puer cum ministro est.
8. Discipulus magistro librum dat.
9. Puer domino cibum dat.
10. stilus domini

6: What case is *oppidum*? nominative
7: Ubi est puer? cum ministro
9: What case is *domino*? dative
9: What case is *cibum*? accusative

Lesson 13a

1. Puer ad cubiculum ambulat.
2. Lupus ad vinum ambulat.
3. Discipulus ante aedificium est.
4. Vir post scutum est.
5. Lupus post baculum est.
6. Telum super oppidum est.
7. Caelum super oppidum est.
8. Vinum apud poculum est.
9. Puer domino cibum dat.
10. Dominus servo calceum dat.

6: What case is *telum*? nominative
7: What case is *oppidum*? accusative
8: Quid est apud poculum? vinum
9: Quis domino cibum dat? puer

Lesson 13b

1. Lupus ad vinum ambulat.
2. Astrum super oppidum est.
3. Aedificium apud saxum est.
4. Astrum in caelo est.
5. Telum in caelo est.
6. Discipulus ab aedificio ambulat.
7. Capillus in lupo est.
8. Puer domino cibum dat.
9. Dominus filio calceum dat.
10. telum servi

2: Quid super oppidum est? astrum
6: Unde discipulus ambulat? ab aedificio
8: What case is *puer*? nominative
10: What case is *servi*? genitive

Lesson 14a

1. Puer bracchium pulsat.
2. Puer scutum pulsat.
3. Puer poculum sumit.
4. Puer pirum sumit.
5. Puer nummum sumit.
6. Puer poculum ponit.
7. Puer pirum ponit.
8. Puer nummum ponit.
9. Puer donum iacit.
10. Puer telum iacit.

3: Quid puer sumit? poculum
7: Quis pirum ponit? puer
9: What case is *donum*? accusative
9: What case is *puer*? nominative

Lesson 14b

1. Puer nasum pulsat.
2. Puer saxum pulsat.
3. Puer astrum videt.
4. Puer malum habet.
5. Vir post scutum est.
6. Puer cultrum sumit.
7. Puer pullum capit.
8. Puer ad cubiculum ambulat.
9. Puer ad donum ambulat.
10. Equus in oppido est.

1: Quis nasum pulsat? puer
7: Quid puer capit? pullum
9: Quo puer ambulat? ad donum
10: Ubi est equus? in oppido

Lesson 15a

1. Minister astro pullum dat.
2. Discipulus saxo gladium dat.
3. Discipulus saxo folium dat.
4. Deus caelo astrum dat.
5. Puer domino cibum dat.
6. Puer servo cibum dat.
7. Puer oppido donum dat.
8. Puer ovum capit.
9. Puer in speculo est.
10. Discipulus ex aedificio ambulat.

1: Quis astro pullum dat? minister
3: Quid discipulus saxo dat? folium
8: Quid puer capit? ovum
10: Unde discipulus ambulat? ex aedificio

Lesson 15b

1. Minister astro pirum dat.
2. Deus caelo astrum dat.
3. Puer domino cibum dat.
4. ovum pueri
5. Puer ministro cultrum dat.
6. Discipulus ab aedificio ambulat.
7. Discipulus ad aedificium ambulat.
8. Lupus ab fluvio ambulat.
9. Lupus ad fluvium ambulat.
10. Asinus in tecto est.

6: Unde discipulus ambulat? ab aedificio
7: Quo discipulus ambulat? ad aedificium
8: Unde lupus ambulat? ab fluvio
9: Quo lupus ambulat? ad fluvium

Lesson 16a

1. gladius monstri
2. lignum monstri
3. saccus monstri
4. gladii monstri
5. gladius domini
6. vestigium ursi
7. Puer telum iacit.
8. Puer lignum capit.
9. Minister monstro pirum dat.
10. Puer ad cubiculum ambulat.

1: What case is *monstri*? genitive
1: What case is *gladius*? nominative
7: Quid puer capit? accusative
10: Quo puer ambulat? ad cubiculum

Lesson 16b

1. saccus monstri
2. gladii monstri
3. lignum monstri
4. vestigium lupi
5. Puer in bello est.
6. Puer malum habet.
7. Monstrum post ostium est.
8. Minister monstro pirum dat.
9. Monstrum in balneo est.
10. Puer ad balneum ambulat.

4: What case is *vestigium*? nominative
5: Quis malum habet? puer
9: Ubi est monstrum? in balneo
10: Quo ambulat puer? ad balneum

Lesson 17a

1. bacula
2. vestimenta
3. monstra
4. Vocabula
5. ova
6. pira
7. oculi
8. gladii
9. pueri
10. cultri

Is *vestimentum* singular or plural? singular
Is *vestimenta* singular or plural? plural
Is *puer* singular or plural? singular
Is *cultri* singular or plural? plural

Lesson 17b

1. Monstra in balneo sunt.
2. Bacula in fluvio sunt.
3. Mala in campo sunt.
4. Gladii in horto sunt.
5. Pueri sub balneo sunt.
6. Puer ante hortum est.
7. Pueri ante hortum sunt.
8. Lupus super hortum est.
9. Lupi super hortum sunt.
10. gladius monstri

1: Ubi sunt monstra? in balneo
3: Ubi sunt mala? in campo
9: What case is *lupi*? nominative
10: What case is *monstri*? genitive

Lesson 18a

1. Puella in insulā est.
2. Femina ex villā ambulat.
3. Puer sub mensā est.
4. Puer de bello cogitat.
5. Puer de puellā cogitat.
6. Lupus ex horto ambulat.
7. Femina ex horto ambulat.
8. bacula
9. puellae
10. pira

1: What case is *puella*? nominative
1: What case is *insulā*? ablative
7: Quis ex horto ambulat? femina
10: Is *pira* singular or plural? plural

Lesson 18b

1. Puella in viā est.
2. Femina ex viā ambulat.
3. Puer sub sellā est.
4. Puella sub astro est.
5. puellae
6. sellae
7. Sellae in caelo sunt.
8. Puer cum puellā est.
9. Puer de libro cogitat.
10. Puer de puellā cogitat.

1: Ubi est puella? in viā
2: Unde femina ambulat? ex viā
3: What case is *sellā*? ex sellā
7: What case is *sellae*? nominative

Lesson 19a

1. Femina ad villam ambulat.
2. Femina ad saxum ambulat.
3. Lupus super lunam est.
4. Lupus super sellam est.
5. Familia apud villam est.
6. Familia apud hortum est.
7. Femina per ianuam (ostium) ambulat.
8. Lupus per fluvium ambulat.
9. Puellae in insulā sunt.
10. Bacula in insulā sunt.

1: Quo femina ambulat? ad villam
3: Ubi est lupus? super lunam
9: What case is *puellae*? nominative
10: Is *bacula* singular or plural? plural

Lesson 19b

1. Femina ad puellam ambulat.
2. Femina ad templum ambulat.
3. Puella post ianuam est.
4. Monstrum post ianuam est.
5. Puella ante ianuam est.
6. Femina per ianuam ambulat.
7. Lupus per fluvium ambulat.
8. Puer per ventum ambulat.
9. linguae
10. Puer sub mensā est.

2: Quis ad templum ambulat? femina
4: What case is *ianuam*? accusative
9: Is *linguae* singular or plural? plural
10: Ubi est puer? sub mensā

Lesson 20a

1. Puella villam amat.
2. Puella ludum amat.
3. Puella agrum amat.
4. Puer donum fert.
5. Puer clipeum fert.
6. Puella in triclinio plorat.
7. Puella in viā ridet.
8. Puer ab horto currit.
9. Puer ad hortum currit.
10. Puella feminam amat.

2: Quid puella amat? ludum
5: Quis clipeum fert? puer
8: Unde puer currit? ab horto
9: Quo puer currit? ad hortum

Lesson 20b

1. Puella lunam amat.
2. Puer lunam timet.
3. Puer monstrum timet.
4. Puer bellum timet.
5. Puer medicum timet.
6. Monstra in viā sunt.
7. Puer ad aedificium currit.
8. Puer ex aedificio currit.
9. Puellae in insulā sunt.
10. Pueri in lunā sunt.

5: Quis medicum timet? puer
6: Ubi sunt monstra? in viā
7: Quo puer currit? ad aedificium
8: Unde puer currit? ex aedificio

Lesson 21a

1. Nuntius feminae epistulam dat.
2. Nuntius feminae pilam dat.
3. Servus reginae coronam dat.
4. Discipulus puellae paginam dat.
5. Discipulus puellae lignum dat.
6. Puer servo gladium dat.
7. Puer rosam fert.
8. Puer ad hortum currit.
9. Puer ab horto currit.
10. Puer ab flammā currit.

1: Quid nuntius feminae dat? epistulam
3: Quis reginae coronam dat? servus
5: What case is *puellae*? dative
10: Unde puer currit? ab flammā

Lesson 21b

1. Servus reginae lunam dat.
2. Discipulus flammae lignum dat.
3. Puella in triclinio ridet.
4. Puella in viā plorat.
5. Lupus super sellam est.
6. Lupus super flammam est.
7. Lupus super fluvium est.
8. Familia apud villam est.
9. Puer apud flammam est.
10. rosae

1: Quis reginae lunam dat? servus
4: Ubi puella ridet? in viā
7: Ubi est lupus? super fluvium
10: What case is *rosae*? nominative

Lesson 22a

1. rosa puellae
2. tabula puellae
3. penna aquilae
4. epistula aquilae
5. tabula servi
6. tabula monstri
7. Puer caudam habet.
8. lignum monstri
9. Nuntius feminae epistulam dat.
10. vestigium ursi

1: What case is *puellae*? genitive
1: What case is *rosa*? nominative
8: What case is *monstri*? genitive
8: What case is *lignum*? nominative

Lesson 22b

1. telum puellae
2. pullus puellae
3. ovum aquilae
4. Magister sub saxo est.
5. sellae
6. pulli
7. folia
8. Sellae in campo sunt.
9. Pulli in triclinio sunt.
10. Folia in ramo sunt.

1: What case is *puellae*? genitive
3: What case is *ovum*? nominative
7: Is *folia* singular or plural? plural
10: Ubi sunt folia? plural

Lesson 23a

1. agni
2. Puer cum servo est.
3. Lupus sub petaso est.
4. Puer domino cibum dat.
5. Dominus delphino calceum dat.
6. pugnus pueri
7. Discipulus saxo gladium dat.
8. gladius monstri
9. Puer sub mensā est.
10. Servus reginae coronam dat.

2: Ubi est puer? cum servo
5: Quid dominus delphino dat? calceum
8: What case is *monstri*? genitive
9: What case is *mensā*? ablative

Lesson 23b

1. Agnus in campo est.
2. Puer ad focum ambulat.
3. Puer ad saxum ambulat.
4. Puer monstro rosam dat.
5. labra
6. Vinum apud poculum est.
7. Puellae in viā sunt.
8. Femina ad villam ambulat.
9. Discipulus puellae paginam dat.
10. pennae aquilae

4: Quis monstro rosam dat? puer
6: What case is *poculum*? accusative
8: Quo femina ambulat? ad villam
10: What case is *aquilae*? genitive

Lesson 24a
1. Puer cum monstris est.
2. Puer cum monstro est.
3. Puer cum puellis est.
4. Puer cum puellā est.
5. Puer de porcis cogitat.
6. Puer de porco cogitat.
7. Puer ab araneis currit.
8. Puer ab araneā currit.
9. Monstra in balneis sunt.
10. Monstrum in balneo est.

1: Is *monstris* singular or plural? plural
2: Is *monstro* singular or plural? singular
7: Is *araneis* singular or plural? plural
8: Is *araneā* singular or plural? singular

Lesson 24b
1. Puer cum monstro est.
2. Puer cum monstris est.
3. Puer de signo cogitat.
4. Puer de signis cogitat.
5. Pueri sub mensis sunt.
6. Pueri sub sellis sunt.
7. Puellae in lectis sunt.
8. Puellae in hortis sunt.
9. Coloni in agris sunt.
10. Puer ab ursis ambulat.

1: What case is *monstro*? ablative
2: What case is *monstris*? ablative (plural)
6: What case is *sellis*? ablative (plural)
9: What case is *agris*? ablative (plural)

Lesson 25a
1. Puer ad gallos ambulat.
2. Puer ad gallum ambulat.
3. Tabernarius ante ursos est.
4. Tabernarius ante ursum est.
5. Puer ad horologia ambulat.
6. Puer ad horologium ambulat.
7. Femina ad villas ambulat.
8. Femina ad villam ambulat.
9. Lupus super sellas est.
10. Lupus super sellam est.

1: What number is *gallos*? plural
2: What number is *gallum*? singular
5: What number is *horologia*? plural
6: What number is *horologium*? singular

Lesson 25b
1. Puer ad calceos ambulat.
2. Lupus super saxa est.
3. Puella ante flammas est.
4. Lupus super sellam est.
5. Lupi super sellas sunt.
6. Lupus super sellas est.
7. digiti
8. bacula
9. feminae
10. Monstra in balneis sunt.

1: What case is *calceos*? accusative (plural)
3: What case is *flammas*? accusative (plural)
7: What number is *digiti*? plural
8: What number is *bacula*? plural

Lesson 26a
1. Puer deos vocat.
2. Puer deum vocat.
3. Puella hortos vult.
4. Puella hortum vult.
5. Dominus monstra iubet.
6. Dominus monstrum iubet.
7. Puella sagittas audit.
8. Puella sagittam audit.
9. Puer regulas monstrat.
10. Puer regulam monstrat.

1: Quis deos vocat? puer
3: Quid puella vult? hortos
7: Quis sagittas audit? puella
8: Quid puella audit? sagittam

Lesson 26b
1. Puer deos timet.
2. Puer monstra timet.
3. Puer puellas timet.
4. Dominus medicos iubet.
5. Dominus astra iubet.
6. Dominus feminas iubet.
7. Tabernarius ante ursos est.
8. Puer ad gallos ambulat.
9. Puer ab araneis currit.
10. Puer de rosis cogitat.

1: Quid puer timet? deos
2: What case is *monstra*? accusative (plural)
7: Ubi est tabernarius? ante ursos
9: Unde puer currit? ab araneis

Lesson 27a

1. Puer dominis cibum dat.
2. Puer domino cibum dat.
3. Puer cocis malum dat.
4. Puer coco malum dat.
5. Puer cocis mala dat.
6. Puella sepulcris rosam dat.
7. Puella sepulcro rosam dat.
8. Puella sepulcris rosas dat.
9. Puella sepulcro rosas dat.
10. Puer de porcis cogitat.

1: What case is *puer*? nominative
2: What case is *domino*? dative
3: What case is *cibum*? accusative
5: What number is *cocis*? plural

Lesson 27b

1. Puer coco cultrum dat.
2. Puer cocis cultros dat.
3. Puella sepulcris rosam dat.
4. Minister astris pullum dat.
5. Nuntius feminis epistulam dat.
6. Nuntius feminae epistulam dat.
7. coci
8. sepulcra
9. stellae
10. Puellae in lectis sunt.

1: Quid puer coco dat? dative
4: Quis astris pullum dat? minister
7: What case is *coci*? nominative (plural)
10: Ubi sunt puellae? in lectis

Lesson 28a

1. linea puerorum
2. linea pueri
3. linea monstrorum
4. linea monstri
5. linea puellarum
6. linea puellae
7. gladius domini
8. gladius dominorum
9. rosa puellarum
10. rosae puellarum

1: What number is *puerorum*? plural
2: What number is *pueri*? singular
6: What number is *puellae*? singular
9: What number is *puellarum*? plural

Lesson 28b

1. gemma puellae
2. gemma pueri
3. gemma monstri
4. gemma puellarum
5. gemma puerorum
6. gemma monstrorum
7. telum domini
8. telum dominorum
9. tela domini
10. tela dominorum

1: What case is *gemma*? nominative
1: What case is *puellae*? genitive
10: What case is *tela*? nominative (plural)
10: What case is *dominorum*? genitive (plural)

Lesson 29a

1. Puer dominum pulsat.
2. Pueri dominum pulsant.
3. Puella in viā ridet.
4. Puellae in viā rident.
5. Tabernarius gemmam vendit.
6. Tabernarii gemmas vendunt.
7. Puer in campo dormit.
8. Pueri in campo dormiunt.
9. Puer templum ascendit.
10. Pueri templum ascendunt.

1: Is *pulsat* singular or plural? singular
2: Is *pulsant* singular or plural? plural
6: Is *vendunt* singular or plural? plural
9: Is *ascendit* singular or plural? singular

Lesson 29b

1. Puer ad hortum ambulat.
2. Pueri ad hortum ambulant.
3. Puer ad hortos ambulat.
4. Pueri ad hortos ambulant.
5. Puer ab horto ambulat.
6. Pueri ab horto ambulant.
7. Puer ab hortis ambulat.
8. Pueri ab hortis ambulant.
9. Pueri dona iaciunt.
10. Pueri dona capiunt.

4: Quo pueri ambulant? ad hortum
8: Unde pueri ambulant? ab hortis
9: Quid pueri iaciunt? dona
10: Quis dona capit? pueri

Lesson 30a

1. Puer cum cocis est.
2. Puer cum monstris est.
3. Puer ab hortis ambulat.
4. Lupus ad gallos ambulat.
5. Puer ad hortos ambulat.
6. Lupus ad instrumenta ambulat.
7. Lupus ad aedificia ambulat.
8. Lupus ad gemmas ambulat.
9. Femina ad villas ambulat.
10. Puella gallos amat.

1: What case is *cocis*? ablative (plural)
4: What case is *gallos*? accusative (plural)
7: What case is *aedificia*? accusative (plural)
10: What case is *puella*? nominative

Lesson 30b

1. linea puerorum
2. Puer de porcis cogitat.
3. linea puellarum
4. Puer ad hortos ambulat.
5. Puer ab hortis ambulat.
6. linea monstrorum
7. Dominus medicos iubet.
8. Puer servis gladios dat.
9. Puer cocis malum dat.
10. Puellae in lectis sunt.

1: What case is *puerorum*? genitive (plural)
4: Quo puer ambulat? ad hortos
5: Unde puer ambulat? ab hortis
10: Ubi sunt puellae? in lectis

Quiz Answer Key

Vocabula 1
1. campus
2. hortus
3. stilus
4. fluvius
5. puer
6. digitus

7. What part of the body sees? oculus
8. What has flowers or vegetables? hortus

Sententiae 1
1. Puer in campo est.
2. Puer in oculo est.
3. Puer in fluvio est.
4. stili
5. digiti
6. campi

7. Is *horto* normal or ablative? ablative
8. Is *oculi* singular or plural? plural

Vocabula 2
1. stilus
2. mundus
3. dominus
4. lupus
5. murus
6. servus

7. What is long and sharp? gladius
8. What does a *puer* do if he wants to get to someplace? ambulat

Sententiae 2
1. Puer ambulat.
2. oculi
3. digiti
4. lupi
5. Puer cum servo est.
6. Puer cum lupo est.

7. What are three Latin prepositions? in, cum, ab
8. Is *digitus* singular or plural? singular

Vocabula 3A
1. calceus
2. gladius
3. oculus
4. cibus
5. anulus
6. servus

7. What keeps the sun and rain off the head? petasus
8. What carries people and can pull carts? equus

Vocabula 3B
1. equus
2. petasus
3. mundus
4. murus
5. campus
6. stilus

7. What is for eating? cibus
8. What goes on a finger? anulus

Sententiae 3A
1. Lupus sub gladio est.
2. Lupus sub equo est.
3. Lupus sub cibo est.
4. Lupus ex horto ambulat.
5. Puer ex digito ambulat.
6. Puer cum domino est.

7. Give five Latin prepositions. in, cum, ab, ex, sub
8. Is *digito* normal or ablative? ablative

Sententiae 3B
1. Dominus cum lupo est.
2. Puer ab horto ambulat.
2. Puer ab equo ambulat.
4. Lupus in horto est.
5. Lupus in campo est.
6. oculi

7. Is *equi* singular or plural? plural
8. What case is *cibo*? ablative

Vocabula 4A
1. digitus
2. puer
3. (Puer) legit.
4. fluvius
5. calceus
6. mundus

7. What does an author do? scribit
8. What does a horse do all day? stat

Vocabula 4B
1. dominus
2. (Puer) scribit.
3. petasus
4. (Puer) dormit.
5. (Puer) sedet.
6. (Puer) cogitat.

7. What is the Latin word for "world"? mundus
8. What does someone do to a newspaper? legit

Sententiae 4A
1. Puer cogitat.
2. Puer in equo dormit.
3. Puer sub gladio sedet.
4. Puer in campo putat.
5. Puer ab muro ambulat.
6. Lupus sub equo est.
7. Give three Latin verbs. scribit, est, dormit, sedet, cogitat, legit
8. What case is *gladio*? ablative

Sententiae 4B
1. Puer in campo dormit.
2. Puer in equo sedet.
3. Puer in fluvio cogitat.

4. Puer in horto est.
5. Puer ab cibo ambulat.
6. Lupus ex campo ambulat.

7. Is *petasi* singular or plural? plural
8. Give five Latin prepositions. in, cum, ab, ex, sub

Vocabula 5A
1. (Puer) scribit.
2. nasus
3. circulus
4. filius
5. petasus
6. (Puer) stat.

7. What blows through a *campus*? ventus
8. What is the home of a rabbit? cavus

Vocabula 5B
1. dominus
2. ventus
3. anulus
4. cavus
5. capillus
6. digitus

7. What is really, really round? circulus
8. What is in the middle of your face? nasus

Sententiae 5A
1. Puer ante murum est.
2. Puer ante equum est.
3. Puer in fluvio est.
4. Puer in cavo est.
5. Puer ab fluvio ambulat.
6. Puer ab cavo ambulat.

7. What case is *fluvium*? accusative
8. Give two prepositions that take the accusative case? ad, ante

Sententiae 5B
1. Lupus sub gladio est.
2. Lupus sub capillo est.
3. Puer in fluvio cogitat.
4. Puer in cavo cogitat.
5. Lupus ad capillum ambulat.
6. Lupus ad fluvium ambulat.

7. What case is *cavum*? accusative
8. What case is *cavo*? ablative

Vocabula 6A
1. ventus
2. asinus
3. fluvius
4. murus
5. oculus
6. ursus

7. What belongs in a *sacculus*? nummus
8. Who has a wife? maritus

Vocabula 6B
1. calceus
2. circulus
3. anulus
4. nummus
5. saccus
6. mundus

7. What animal sleeps in a *cavus*? ursus
8. What animal brays, "Hee haw"? asinus

Sententiae 6A
1. Lupus post campus est.
2. Lupus super hortum est.
3. Puer apud saccum est.
4. Puer ad hortum ambulat.
5. Puer ad nasum ambulat.
6. Equus ante murum est.

7. Give five prepositions that take the accusative case. ad, ante, post, super, apud
8. Give five prepositions that take the ablative case. in, cum, ab, ex, sub

Vocabula 7A
1. (Puer) videt.
2. nummus
3. petasus
4. saccus
5. cibus
6. (Puer) legit.

7. What is a *lupus*'s favorite *cibus*? agnus
8. What loves to play in the ocean? delphinus

Sententiae 7A
1. Puer murum pulsat.
2. Puer nasum pulsat.
3. Puer mundum pulsat.
4. Puer lupum videt.
5. Puer calceum videt.
6. Puer cibum habet.

7. What case does a direct object have? accusative
8. What case does *in* take? ablative

Vocabula 8A
1. ursus
2. ventus
3. medicus
4. gladius
5. nuntius
6. stilus

7. What comes out of an egg? pullus
8. What connects the arm to the body? umerus

Sententiae 8A
1. Puer servo cibum dat.
2. Puer equo cibum dat.
3. Dominus servo calceum dat.
4. Servus lupo cibum dat.
5. Puer dominum pulsat.
6. Puer nasum videt.

7. What is the dative case used for? indirect object
8. What case is used for the direct object? accusative

Sententiae 6B
1. Lupus post cavum est.
2. Lupus super fluvium est.
3. Puer apud fluvium est.
4. Puer ad equum ambulat.
5. Puer ante hortum est.
6. Puer in campo dormit.

7. Give five prepositions that take the accusative case. ad, ante, post, super, apud
8. Give five prepositions that take the ablative case. in, cum, ab, ex, sub

Vocabula 7B
1. (Puer) pulsat.
2. equus
3. capillus
4. (Puer) habet.
5. campus
6. amicus

7. What is a round piece of money? nummus
8. What does someone do at night? dormit

Sententiae 7B
1. Puer calceum habet.
2. Puer cum lupo est.
3. Lupus in campo est.
4. Equus in campo est.
5. Puer in fluvio cogitat.
6. Puer sub sacco cogitat.

7. What case is *nasum*? accusative
8. What case is *naso*? ablative

Vocabula 8B
1. umerus
2. deus
3. calceus
4. digitus
5. pullus
6. murus

7. Who brings a letter? nuntius
8. What heats things up? focus

Sententiae 8B
1. Puer lupo cibum dat.
2. Puer servo gladium dat.
3. Dominus lupo calceum dat.
4. Puer murum pulsat.
5. Puer lupum videt.
6. Puer cibum habet.

7. What case is used for the indirect object? dative
8. What case is *lupo* in *Puer lupo calceum dat*? dative

Sententiae 8C
1. Lupus super hortum est.
2. Puer in fluvio est.
3. Puer in horto est.
4. Puer ad hortum ambulat.
5. Puer ab muro ambulat.
6. Puer ab mundo ambulat.

7. Give five prepositions that take the accusative case.
ad, ante, post, super, apud
8. What two cases could *muro* be? ablative or dative

Vocabula 9A
1. medicus
2. nidus
3. nasus
4. rivus
5. ventus
6. ramus

7. What is a home for birds? nidus
8. What is "three"? numerus

Vocabula 9B
1. nuntius
2. numerus
3. capillus
4. saccus
5. oceanus
6. umerus

7. What holds up a *nidus*? ramus
8. What is a little *fluvius*? rivus

Sententiae 9A
1. gladius domini
2. cibus domini
3. pullus domini
4. gladius servi
5. anulus servi
6. cibus lupi

7. What case is *nuntii* in *saccus nuntii*? genitive
8. Give five cases that take the ablative case. in, cum, ab, ex, sub

Sententiae 9B
1. Dominus servo calceum dat.
2. Puer servo gladium dat.
3. Puer fluvio cibum dat.
4. Puer domino cibum dat.
5. Puer in horto est.
6. Puer ab horto ambulat.

7. What two cases could *servo* be? dative or ablative
8. What case does *cum* take? ablative

Sententiae 9C
1. Puer ex horto ambulat.
2. Puer ad hortum ambulat.
3. Puer ante hortum est.
4. calcei
5. oculi
6. Ursus post saccum est.

7. What two cases could *horto* be? ablative or dative
8. What case is *ursi* in *cibus ursi*? genitive

Vocabula 10A
1. nidus
2. vir
3. circulus
4. clipeus
5. amicus
6. oceanus

7. Who learns in a *ludus*? discipulus
8. What is a hand closed up tight? pugnus

Vocabula 10B
1. pugnus
2. discipulus
3. ramus
4. rivus
5. (Puer) putat.
6. ludus

7. What blocks a sword or spear? clipeus
8. Who grows crops in a field? colonus

Sententiae 10A
1. Lupus ab viro ambulat.
2. Puer virum pulsat.
3. Puer viro cibum dat.
4. pullus pueri
5. pueri
6. dominus servi

7. What two cases could *domino* be? dative or ablative
8. What case is *ramum*? accusative

Sententiae 10B
1. Lupus ad virum ambulat.
2. Puer domino clipeum dat.
3. Dominus puero calceum dat.
4. Puer ad ludum ambulat.
5. viri
6. Gladius in clipeo est.

7. What case is *pullus*? nominative
8. What case is *pullum*? accusative

Sententiae 10C
1. Puer ante murum est.
2. Puer in muro est.
3. Puer ab muro ambulat.
4. Puer murum pulsat.
5. Lupus post saccum est.
6. Ursus post saccum est.

7. What case is *murus*? nominative
8. What is the nominative case used for? subject

Vocabula 11A
1. ager
2. culter
3. minister
4. ramus
5. rivus
6. vir

7. Who teaches? magister
8. What is hairy and has sharp tusks? aper

Vocabula 11B
1. magister
2. liber
3. pugnus
4. ludus
5. clipeus
6. discipulus

7. What cuts food? culter
8. What is a place where crops grow? ager

Sententiae 11A
1. Colonus in agro est.
2. Minister in cultro est.
3. Lupus post librum est.
4. Lupus ab cultro ambulat.
5. Puer murum pulsat.
6. Puer ministrum pulsat.

7. What is the accusative of *ager*? agrum
8. What is the ablative of *liber*? libro

Sententiae 11B
1. Puer domino cibum dat.
2. Puer viro clipeum dat.
3. Discipulus magistro librum dat.
4. Puer ministro cultrum dat.
5. Puer servo cultrum dat.
6. gladius domini

7. What is the genitive of *minister*? ministri
8. What two cases could *magistro* be? ablative or dative

Sententiae 11C
1. gladius servi
2. pugnus pueri
3. culter ministri
4. oculi
5. cultri
6. libri

7. What is the ablative of *culter*? cultro
8. What two cases could *agri* be? nominative (pl) or genitive (sg)

Vocabula 12A
1. baculum
2. aedificium
3. collum
4. ventus
5. oppidum
6. tergum

7. What connects a hand to a *umerus*? bracchium
8. What is hard and sticks up out of the ground? saxum

Vocabula 12B
1. umerus
2. minister
3. bracchium
4. saccus
5. ludus
6. saxum

7. What is always behind you? tergum
8. What has walls, windows, and doors? aedificium

Sententiae 12A
1. Puer in aedificio est.
2. Magister in bracchio est.
3. Digitus in naso est.
4. Discipulus ab aedificio ambulat.
5. Discipulus ab baculo ambulat.
6. Puer sub bracchio stat.

7. What case could *aedificium* be? nominative (or accusative)
8. What case could *baculo* be? ablative (or dative)

Sententiae 12B
1. Saxum in oppido est.
2. Minister in cultro est.
3. Discipulus ex aedificio ambulat.
4. Discipulus ~~ambulat~~ ab saxo ambulat.
5. Puer sub baculo stat.
6. Puer sub saxo stat.

7. What case could *saxum* be? nominative (or accusative)
8. What case could *saxo* be? ablative (or dative).

Sententiae 12C
1. Magister sub saxo est.
2. gladius domini
3. baculum domini
4. Puer viro cibum dat.
5. Puer ministro cultrum dat.
6. oculi

7. What case is *puer*? nominative
8. What cases could *viro* be? ablative (or dative)

Vocabula 13A
1. collum
2. bracchium
3. tergum
4. vinum
5. cubiculum
6. scutum

7. What is in the *caelum* at night? astrum
8. What is like a *scutum*, but round? clipeus

Vocabula 13B
1. caelum
2. asinus
3. astrum
4. telum
5. poculum
6. capillus

7. What holds *vinum*? poculum
8. What is the place where someone *dormit*? cubiculum

Sententiae 13A
1. Puer ad cubiculum ambulat.
2. Lupus ad vinum ambulat.
3. Vir ante scutum est.
4. Vir post scutum est.
5. Telum super oppidum est.
6. Vinum apud poculum est.

7. What two cases could *cubiculum* be? nominative or accusative
8. Give five prepositions that take the accusative case? ad, ante, post, super, apud

Sententiae 13B
1. Scutum apud telum est.
2. Astrum in caelo est.
3. Puer in saxo est.
4. Discipulus ad aedificium ambulat.
5. Discipulus ex aedificio ambulat.
6. Discipulus ab aedificio ambulat.

7. What case is *ministri* in *culter ministri*? genitive
8. What case is *domino* in *Puer domino cibum dat*? dative

Sententiae 13C
1. Discipulus ante aedificium est.
2. scutum servi
3. telum domini
4. poculum domini
5. Puer domino cibum dat.
6. Puer in aedificio est.

7. What case is *servi* in *cibus servi*? genitive
8. What is the dative case used for? indirect object

Vocabula 14A
1. (Puer) sumit.
2. pugnus
3. pirum
4. caelum
5. (Puer) ponit.
6. malum

7. What does a person do to a *telum*? iacit
8. What does a person get on a birthday? donum

Vocabula 14B
1. donum
2. (Puer) capit.
3. (Puer) iacit.
4. collum
5. ludus
6. ramus

7. What does fisherman do to fish? capit
8. What is like a *pirum* but rounder? malum

Sententiae 14A
1. Puer bracchium pulsat.
2. Puer aedificium pulsat.
3. Puer cultrum sumit.
4. Puer pirum ponit.
5. Puer pullum iacit.
6. Puer donum capit.

7. What case is *saxum* in *puer saxum habet*? accusative
8. What case is *pirum* in *pirum in puero est*? nominative

Sententiae 14B
1. Puer murum pulsat.
2. Puer donum sumit.
3. Puer pirum sumit.
4. Puer poculum ponit.
5. Puer pullum capit.
6. Puer cibum habet.

7. What case is *donum* in *donum in fluvio est*? nominative
8. What case is *cibum*? accusative

Sententiae 14C
1. Puer malum habet.
2. gladius servi
3. culter ministri
4. Puer lupo cibum dat.
5. Puer servo pirum dat.
6. libri

7. What case is *pullum*? accusative
8. What case is *poculum* in *poculum in campo est*? nominative

Vocabula 15A
1. bellum
2. folium
3. scutum
4. ovum
5. speculum
6. poculum

7. What is a yellow metal? aurum
8. What is a silver metal? argentum

Vocabula 15B
1. ager
2. (Puer) ponit.
3. clipeus
4. pugnus
5. tectum
6. (Puer) sumit.

7. What happens when two countries fight? bellum
8. What holds a *pullus* before it hatches? ovum

Sententiae 15A

1. Puer oppido donum dat.
2. Discipulus saxo gladium dat.
3. Minister astro pullum dat.
4. Deus caelo astrum dat.
5. Puer ministro cultrum dat.
6. Puer servo pirum dat.

7. What case is *minister*? nominative
8. What two cases could *clipeo* be? dative or ablative

Sententiae 15B

1. Puer domino cibum dat.
2. Puer lupo cibum dat.
3. Discipulus magistro librum dat.
4. Puer pullum iacit.
5. Puer donum capit.
6. culter ministri

7. What two cases could *caelum* be? nominative or accusative
8. What is the dative case used for? indirect object

Sententiae 15C

1. ovum pueri
2. Astrum in speculo est.
3. Asinus in tecto est.
4. Lupus ex fluvio ambulat.
5. Lupus ab fluvio ambulat.
6. Lupus ad fluvium ambulat.

7. What case could *ovum* be? nominative or accusative
8. What two things is the accusative used for? direct object and prepositions

Vocabula 16A

1. bellum
2. lignum
3. ostium
4. vocabulum
5. balneum
6. folium

7. What is really, really scary? monstrum
8. What does a foot leave behind? vestigium

Vocabula 16B

1. vestigium
2. monstrum
3. tectum
4. tergum
5. ovum
6. (Puer) cogitat.

7. What burns in a fire? lignum
8. What leads in and out of an *aedificium*? ostium

Sententiae 16A

1. gladius monstri
2. saccus monstri
3. pullus monstri
4. stilus domini
5. vestigium ursi
6. Puer murum pulsat.

7. What case is *stilus*? nominative
8. What case is *ursi*? genitive

Sententiae 16B

1. Puer lupum videt.
2. Puer lignum capit.
3. Puer murum pulsat.
4. Lupum puer videt.
5. Lignum puer capit.
6. Puer domino cibum dat.

What two cases could *lignum* be? nominative and accusative
What two cases could *vestigio* be? dative and ablative

Sententiae 16C

1. Puer lupo cibum dat.
2. Domino puer cibum dat.
3. Minister monstro mundum dat.
4. Monstrum in balneo est.
5. Puer ad balneum ambulat.
6. stili

7. What case does *cum* take? ablative
8. What case does *apud* take? accusative

Vocabula 17A
1. osculum
2. cerebrum
3. ostium
4. vestigium
5. nummus
6. vestimentum

7. What is the place where people eat dinner? triclinium
8. What is on the outside of the mouth? labrum

Vocabula 17B
1. labrum
2. vocabulum
3. lignum
4. templum
5. filius
6. triclinium

7. What does someone wear? vestimentum
8. What should someone give to their mother often? osculum

Sententiae 17A
1. bacula
2. monstra
3. mala
4. Astra in caelo sunt.
5. Monstra in balneo sunt.
6. Gladii in horto sunt.

7. Is *oppida* singular or plural? plural
8. Is *aedificium* singular or plural? singular

Sententiae 17B
1. vestimenta
2. pira
3. pocula
4. Mala in campo sunt.
5. Pueri in horto sunt.
6. Asini in tecto sunt.

7. Is *sunt* singular or plural? plural
8. Is *malum* singular or plural? singular

Sententiae 17C
1. Viri post scutum sunt.
2. Lupi super hortum sunt.
3. Monstra in templo sunt.
4. gladius monstri
5. Puer murum pulsat.
6. Puer donum iacit.

7. What two cases could *donum* be? nominative or accusative
8. What is the nominative case used for? subject

Vocabula 18A
1. osculum
2. insula
3. puella
4. femina
5. via
6. templum

7. What holds *cibus* off the ground? mensa
8. What holds a sitting person off the ground? sella

Vocabula 18B
1. mensa
2. villa
3. petasus
4. labrum
5. sella
6. triclinium

7. What is a *puella* all grown up? femina
8. What leads from one *oppidum* to another? via

Sententiae 18A
1. Puella in insulā est.
2. Puella in viā est.
3. Puella in villā est.
4. Lupus ex horto ambulat.
5. Lupus ex viā ambulat.
6. Lupus ex villā ambulat.

7. What case is *viā*? ablative
8. What case is *via*? nominative

Sententiae 18B
1. Femina ab villā ambulat.
2. Puer sub mensā est.
3. Pueri sub mensā sunt.
4. Puer sub sellā est.
5. puellae
6. Puer cum puellā est.

7. What case is *mensa*? nominative
8. What case is *mensā*? ablative

Sententiae 18C

1. Puer de libro cogitat.
2. Puer de calceo cogitat.
3. scuta
4. Monstra in balneo sunt.
5. Pueri sub balneo sunt.
6. mensa monstri

7. What case is *femina*? nominative
8. What case is *feminā*? ablative

Vocabula 19A

1. ursus
2. astrum
3. domina
4. ianua
5. lingua
6. ventus

7. What leads into an *oppidum* through a *murus*?
8. What looks bigger than an *astrum* in the *caelum* at night?

Vocabula 19B

1. luna
2. familia
3. dominus
4. filia
5. porta
6. triclinium

7. What tastes *cibus*? lingua
8. What is a *femina* who is in charge of a house? domina

Sententiae 19A

1. Femina ad villam ambulat.
2. Femina ad viam ambulat.
3. Lupus super petasum est.
4. Puella ante lunam est.
5. Familia apud villam est.
6. Femina per ianuam ambulat.

7. What case is *feminam*? accusative
8. What case is *puellā*? ablative

Sententiae 19B

1. Femina ad puellam ambulat.
2. Lupus super lunam est.
3. Puella ante ianuam est.
4. Puella post lunam est.
5. Familia apud viam est.
6. Lupus per fluvium ambulat.

7. What case is *ianuam*? accusative
8. What case is *via*? nominative

Sententiae 19C

1. Puella in insulā est.
2. Puellae in insulā sunt.
3. Puer de lunā cogitat.
4. vestimenta
5. vestigia
6. stilus pueri

7. What two cases could *pueri* be? genitive or nominative (plural)
8. What two cases could *vestimentum* be? nominative or accusative

Vocabula 20A

1. (Puella) plorat.
2. (Puer) timet.
3. (Puer) legit.
4. (Puer) fert.
5. (Puer) currit.
6. porta

7. What is land surrounded by water? insula
8. What is a *femina* before she grows up? puella

Vocabula 20B

1. nummus
2. (Puella) amat.
3. lingua
4. nidus
5. anulus
6. (Puella) ridet.

7. What is a place where a *deus* is worshipped? templum
8. What part of the body *cogitat*? cerebrum

Sententiae 20A

1. Puella feminam amat.
2. Puella lunam amat.
3. Puella insulam amat.
4. Puella ludum amat.
5. Puella monstrum amat.
6. Puer donum fert.

7. What case is *lunam*? accusative
8. What case shows possession? genitive

Sententiae 20B

1. Puer bellum timet.
2. Puer medicum timet.
3. Puer puellam timet.
4. Puer sellam sumit.
5. Puer sellam ponit.
6. Puella in triclinio plorat.
7. What case is *medicum*? accusative
8. What two cases could *oppido* be? dative or ablative

Sententiae 20C

1. Puella in triclinio ridet.
2. Puer ad hortum currit.
3. Puer ab horto currit.
4. puellae
5. Monstra in viā sunt.
6. Pueri in insulā sunt.

7. Is *sunt* singular or plural? plural
8. Is *monstra* singular or plural? plural

Vocabula 21A

1. (Puella) plorat.
2. regina
3. flamma
4. capillus
5. rosa
6. pagina

7. What is carried by a *nuntius*? epistula
8. What is worn on the head of a *regina*? corona

Vocabula 21B

1. epistula
2. (Puer) fert.
3. corona
4. (Puella) amat.
5. ostium
6. pila

7. What *femina* wears a *corona*? regina
8. What is very, very hot? flamma

Sententiae 21A

1. Servus reginae coronam dat.
2. Nuntius feminae pilam dat.
3. Vir feminae rosam dat.
4. Puella rosam amat.
5. Puer calceum habet.
6. Puer astrum videt.

7. What is the dative case of *luna*? lunae
8. What is the accusative case of luna? lunam

Sententiae 21B

1. Puer reginae coronam dat.
2. Puer servo pirum dat.
3. Discipulus monstro pullum dat.
4. Puella monstrum amat.
5. Minster cultrum habet.
6. Puer flammam videt.

7. What case is used for the direct object? accusative
8. What case is used to show possession? genitive

Sententiae 21C

1. Femina ad hortum ambulat.
2. Femina ad villam ambulat.
3. Lupus super lunam est.
4. oculi
5. bacula
6. feminae

7. What case is used for the indirect object? dative
8. What case is used for the subject? nominative

Vocabula 22A

1. deus
2. dea
3. fenestra
4. tabula
5. penna
6. cauda

7. What has *pennae* and flies in the *caelum*? aquila
8. What is flat and made of wood? tabula

Vocabula 22B

1. pagina
2. aquila
3. corona
4. aqua
5. collum
6. saccus

7. What allows light into an *aedificium*? fenestra
8. What is at the very back of an animal? cauda

Sententiae 22A

1. rosa puellae
2. tabula puellae
3. epistula aquilae
4. gladius monstri
5. petasus servi
6. ovum pueri

7. What two cases could *servi* be? nominative (plural) or genitive
8. What case is *epistula*? nominative

Sententiae 22B

1. Puella discipulo librum dat.
2. Puer lupo caudam dat.
3. Discipulus monstro lignum dat.
4. feminae
5. libri
6. pocula

7. What two cases could *monstro* be? dative or ablative
8. What two cases could *lignum* be? nominative or accusative

Sententiae 22C

1. Asini in tecto sunt.
2. Astra in caelo sunt.
3. Feminae in campo sunt.
4. Puella feminam amat.
5. Puer lunam timet.
6. Puer medicum timet.

7. What is *femina* in the nominative plural? feminae
8. What is *puer* in the nominative plural? pueri

Vocabula 23A

1. femina
2. (Puer) iacit.
3. equus
4. malum
5. corona
6. vestigium

7. What is part of a *liber*? pagina
8. What is thrown back and forth? pila

Vocabula 23B

1. ager
2. amicus
3. (Puella) ridet.
4. ursus
5. cavus
6. fluvius

7. Who works in an *ager*? colonus
8. What is red and grows in a *hortus*? rosa

Sententiae 23A

1. Puer cum lupo est.
2. Discipulus ad aedificium ambulat.
3. Discipulus monstro lignum dat.
4. Puella ante ianuam est.
5. Lupus ab viā ambulat.
6. gladius monstri

7. What case is *villā*? ablative
8. What case is *villam*? accusative

Sententiae 23B

1. Puer lunam timet.
2. pullus puellae
3. asini
4. folia
5. feminae
6. Maritus post campum est.

7. What six prepositions take the ablative case? in, cum, ab, ex, sub, de
8. Is *folia* singular or plural? plural

Sententiae 23C

1. Equus in oppido est.
2. Puer servo gladium dat.
3. Servus reginae lunam dat.
4. Puer pullum iacit.
5. Puer dominum pulsat.
6. cibus servi

7. What five prepositions take the accusative case? ad, ante, post, apud, super
8. Could *servo* be an indirect object or a direct object? indirect object

Vocabula 24A

1. lilium
2. sagitta
3. fenestra
4. signum
5. porcus
6. flamma

7. What has eight legs? aranea
8. What is covered in *pennae*? ala

Vocabula 24B

1. speculum
2. aranea
3. lectus
4. ala
5. cauda
6. epistula

7. What is white and grows in a *hortus*? lilium
8. What is like an *aper* but with less hair? porcus

Sententiae 24A

1. Puer cum monstris est.
2. Puer cum servis est.
3. Puer de porcis cogitat.
4. Puer de astris cogitat.
5. Monstra in balneis sunt.
6. Puellae in lectis sunt.

7. Is *monstro* singular or plural? singular
8. Is *lunis* singular or plural? plural

Sententiae 24B

1. Puer cum lupo est.
2. Puer cum monstro est.
3. Puer cum puellā est.
4. Puellae in hortis sunt.
5. Puella in lecto est.
6. Puer in aedificio est.

7. What is the ablative plural of *lectus*? lectis
8. What three cases could *puellae* be? nominative (plural), genitive, or dative

Sententiae 24C

1. Puer sub balneo est.
2. Puer sub sellā est.
3. Lupus ex horto ambulat.
4. Femina ex horto ambulat.
5. libri
6. linguae

7. What three cases could *sellae* be? nominative (plural), genitive, dative
8. What two cases could *libri* be? nominative (plural) or genitive

Vocabula 25A

1. taberna
2. porcus
3. mendum
4. horologium
5. silva
6. epistula

7. Who sells things? tabernarius
8. What crows in the early morning? gallus

Vocabula 25B

1. aqua
2. tabernarius
3. aranea
4. gallus
5. sagitta
6. regula

7. What has lots of trees? silva
8. What shows time? horologium

Sententiae 25A
1. Femina ad villas ambulat.
2. Puer ad hortos ambulat.
3. Puer ad horologium ambulat.
4. Puer ad calceos ambulat.
5. Vinum apud pocula est.
6. Lupus super sellas est.

7. What is the nominative plural of *horologium*? horologia
8. Is *sellas* singular or plural? plural

Sententiae 25B
1. Puer ad horologia ambulat.
2. Femina ad villam ambulat.
3. Puer ad hortum ambulat.
4. Lupus ad aedificia ambulat.
5. Lupus super sellam est.
6. Puella ante lectos est.

7. What two cases could *oppida* be? nominative (plural) or accusative (plural)
8. What case is *viros*? accusative (plural)

Sententiae 25C
1. Puer de porcis cogitat.
2. Puer de mendis cogitat.
3. nasi
4. rosae
5. telum puellae
6. regula puellae

7. What two cases could *telum* be? nominative or accusative
8. What three cases could *viae* be? nominative (plural), genitive, or dative

Vocabula 26A
1. (Dominus) iubet.
2. (Puella) audit.
3. balneum
4. (Puella) vult.
5. (Puer) vocat.
6. (Puer) dicit.

7. What does someone do with their ears? audit
8. What does someone do with their *digitus*? monstrat

Vocabula 26B
1. (Puer) petit.
2. tabernarius
3. silva
4. (Puer) monstrat.
5. fenestra
6. lignum

7. What helps you draw a straight line? regula
8. What does a teacher draw a *circulus* around? mendum

Sententiae 26A
1. Puer deos vocat.
2. Dominus medicos iubet.
3. Puer menda monstrat.
4. Puer tela petit.
5. Puella epistulas vult.
6. Dominus feminas iubet

7. What two cases could *menda* be? nominative (plural) or accusative (plural)
8. What is the ablative plural of *telum*? telis

Sententiae 26B
1. Puer puellam dicit.
2. Puer puellas dicit.
3. Puer saxum dicit.
4. Puer saxa dicit.
5. Puer viros dicit.
6. Puer virum dicit.

7. What three cases could *sellae* be? nominative (plural), genitive, dative
8. What is the accusative plural of *monstrum*? monstra

Sententiae 26C
1. Femina ad villas ambulat.
2. Puer ad gallos ambulat.
3. Vir post scutum est.
4. Vir post scuta est.
5. Puer de rosis cogitat.
6. Puella sub sagittis est.

7. What is the nominative plural of *ager*? agri
8. What is the nominative plural of *scutum*? scuta

Vocabula 27A
1. (Dominus) iubet.
2. (Puer) petit.
3. anima
4. fumus
5. stella
6. (Puer) legit.

7. What is the place someone cooks? culina
8. Who cooks *cibus* for a job? cocus

Sententiae 27A
1. Puer dominis cibum dat.
2. Puella sepulcris rosam dat.
3. Puer coco cultrum dat.
4. Deus animis signum dat.
5. Deus animae signum dat.
6. Puer amicum vocat.

7. What is the dative plural of *puella*? puellis
8. What is the dative singular of *puella*? puellae

Sententiae 27C
1. Puer ad gallos ambulat.
2. Vir post scuta est.
3. Puer cum puellis est.
4. folia
5. rosae
6. lupi

7. What three cases could *rosae* be? nominative (plural), genitive, or dative
8. What case does *apud* take? accusative

Vocabula 28A
1. lectus
2. lacrima
3. gemma
4. instrumentum
5. linea
6. silva

7. What expensive thing is found in a shellfish? margarita
8. What expensive thing is found in a mountain? gemma

Sententiae 28A
1. gemma monstrorum
2. gemma puellarum
3. gemma puerorum
4. gemma monstri
5. gemma puellae
6. gemma pueri

7. What case is *puellarum*? genitive (plural)
8. What is the genitive plural of *fluvius*? fluviorum

Vocabula 27B
1. amica
2. cocus
3. culina
4. sepulcrum
5. gallus
6. regula

7. What rises from *flammae*? fumus
8. What is a place to buy things? taberna

Sententiae 27B
1. Puer cocis cultrum dat.
2. Puer domino cibum dat.
3. Puella sepulcro rosam dat.
4. Deus animis signa dat.
5. Puer amicos vocat.
6. Puer menda monstrat.

7. What two cases could *lunis* be? dative or ablative
8. What two cases could *dei* be? nominative (plural) or genitive

Vocabula 28B
1. titulus
2. anima
3. pretium
4. stella
5. (Puella) ridet.
6. margarita

7. What is a hammer or saw? instrumentum
8. What falls from the *oculus*? lacrima

Sententiae 28B
1. scutum domini
2. Puella ante ianuam est.
3. scutum dominorum
4. scuta dominorum
5. Puella post ianuam est.
6. scuta domini

7. What is the genitive plural of *puer*? puerorum
8. What is the genitive singular of *puer*? pueri

Sententiae 28C

1. Nuntius feminis epistulam dat.
2. Puer dominis cibum dat.
3. Puella epistulas vult.
4. Puer deos vocat.
5. Puer ab araneis currit.
6. Puer ad horologia ambulat.

7. What two cases could *horologia* be? nominative (plural) or accusative (plural)
8. What are six cases that take the ablative case? In, cum, ab, ex, de, sub

Vocabula 29A

1. Puer ascendit.
2. Puer claudit.
3. Puer emit.
4. instrumentum
5. margarita
6. sepulcrum

7. What does a *malum* do when it is ripe? cadit
8. What does a *tabernarius* do? vendit

Vocabula 29B

1. (Puer) aperit.
2. (Puer) descendit.
3. (Tabernarius) vendit.
4. (Puer) cadit.
5. Regula
6. (Puer) monstrat.

7. What does a customer do in a *taberna*? emit
8. What is like a thin rope? linea

Sententiae 29A

1. Puer dominum pulsat.
2. Pueri monstrum pulsant.
3. Pueri ab horto ambulant.
4. Puellae in triclinio rident.
5. Pueri dona iaciunt.
6. Puer ianuam aperit.

7. What would *puer* be in the accusative singular and plural? puerum, pueros
8. What would *puella* be in the accusative singular and plural? puellam, puellas

Sententiae 29B

1. Pueri dominum pulsant.
2. Pueri ad hortum ambulant.
3. Puellae in viā rident.
4. Tabernarii gemmas vendunt.
5. Pueri dona capiunt.
6. Puer ianuam claudit.

7. What two cases could *donis* be? dative or ablative
8. What case is *lunas*? accusative

Sententiae 29C

1. gemma puerorum
2. gemma puellarum
3. tela dominorum
4. Puer de porco cogitat.
5. Puer de porcis cogitat.
6. Puer puellam dicit.

7. What two cases could *pocula* be? nominative or accusative
8. What is the dative plural of *puer*? pueris

Vocabula 30A

1. Puer ascendit.
2. templum
3. regina
4. Puer descendit.
5. capillus
6. sagitta

7. What causes things to be wet? aqua
8. What does a person do when he sees a *monstrum*? timet or currit

Vocabula 30B

1. ramus
2. nasus
3. oppidum
4. instrumentum
5. discipulus
6. nuntius

7. What is good scrambled or fried? ovum
8. What is a place to get clean? balneum

Sententiae 30A

1. Puer cum puellis est.
2. Lupus ad instrumenta ambulat.
3. Pueri de porcis cogitant.
4. Puer ad hortos ambulat.
5. Puer de porcis cogitat.
6. Puer cocis malum dat.

7. What case does *apud* take? accusative
8. What three cases could *linea* be? nominative (plural), genitive, or dative

Sententiae 30B

1. linea puerorum
2. Puella feminas amat.
3. tela dominorum
4. puellae
5. monstra
6. Pueri dominum pulsant.

7. Is *amant* singular or plural? plural
8. What case is *villā*? ablative

Sententiae 30C

1. Maritus post cavum est.
2. Femina ad villas ambulat.
3. Puer cum servo est.
4. Puella ursos amat.
5. telum dominorum
6. pueri

7. What is the genitive plural of *equus*? equorum
8. What is the dative plural of *gallus*? gallis

Latin to English
DICTIONARY

ab (AHB) from, away from, 2
ad (AHD) to, 5
aedificium (aye-di-FI-kee-oom) building, 12
ager (AH-ghayr) field, 11
agnus (AHG-noos) lamb, 7
ala (AH-lah) wing, 24
amat (AH-maht) loves, 20
ambulat (AHM-boo-laht) walks, 2
amica (ah-MEE-kah) friend, 27
amicus (ah-MEE-koos) friend, 7
anima (AH-ni-mah) spirit, 27
ante (AHN-tay) in front of, 5
anulus (AH-noo-loos) ring, 3
aper (AH-payr) boar, 11
aperit (AH-peh-rit) opens, 29
apud (AH-pood) at, 6
aqua (AH-kwah) water, 22
aquila (AH-kwi-lah) eagle, 22
aranea (ah-RAH-neh-ah) spider, 24
argentum (ahr-GHEN-toom) silver, 15
ascendit (ah-SKEHN-dit) climbs up, 29
asinus (AH-see-noos) donkey, 6
astrum (AHS-troom) star, 13
audit (OW-dit) hears, 26
aurum (OW-room) gold, 15
baculum (BAH-koo-loom) stick, 12
balneum (BAHL-neh-oom) bathtub, 16
bellum (BEHL-loom) war, 15
bracchium (BRAHK-ki-oom) arm, 12
cadit (KAH-dit) falls, 29
caelum (KAYE-loom) sky, 13
calceus (KAHL-keh-oos) shoe, 3
campus (KAHM-poos) meadow, 1
capillus (kah-PIL-loos) hair, 5
capit (KAH-pit) catches, 14

cauda (KOW-dah) tail, 22
cavus (KAH-voos) hole, 5
cerebrum (keh-RAY-broom) brain, 17
cibus (KI-boos) food, 3
circulus (KEER-koo-loos) circle, 5
claudit (KLOW-dit) closes, 29
clipeus (KLI-peh-oos) shield, 10
cocus (COH-koos) cook, 27
cogitat (COH-ghee-taht) thinks, 4
collum (KOH-loom) neck, 12
colonus (coh-LOH-noos) farmer, 10
corona (koh-ROH-nah) crown, 21
cubiculum (koo-BI-koo-loom) bedroom, 13
culina (coo-LEE-nah) kitchen, 27
culter (COOL-tayr) knife, 11
cum (KOOM) with, together with, 2
cur? (COOR) why? 16
currit (COOR-rit) runs, 20
de (DAY) about, 18
dea (DAY-ah) goddess, 22
decem (DEH-kehm) ten, 28
delphinus (dehl-FEE-noos) dolphin, 7
descendit (day-SKEHN-dit) goes down, 29
deus (DAY-oos) god, 8
dicit (DEE-kit) says, 26
digitus (DI-ghi-toos) finger, 1
discipulus (di-SKI-poo-loos) student, 10
domina (DOH-mi-nah) mistress, 19
dominus (DOH-mi-noos) master, 2
donum (DOH-noom) present, 14
dormit (DOHR-mit) sleeps, 4
dum (DOOM) while, 4
duo (DOO-oh) two, 9
ecce (EHK-keh) look, 11
emit (EH-mit) buys, 29

121

epistula (eh-PIS-too-lah) letter, 21
equus (EH-kwoos) horse, 3
est (EHST) is, 1
estne (EHST-nay) is it …? 1
et (EHT) and, 3
ex (EHKS) out of, off of, 3
familia (fa-MI-lee-ah) family, 19
femina (FAY-mi-nah) woman, 18
fenestra (feh-NEHS-trah) window, 22
fert (FEHRT) carries, 20
filia (FEE-lee-ah) daughter, 19
filius (FEE-lee-oos) son, 5
finis (FEE-nis) the end, 1
flamma (FLAHM-mah) flame, 21
fluvius (FLOO-vee-oos) river, 1
focus (FOH-koos) cooktop, 8
folium (FOH-lee-oom) leaf, 15
fumus (FOO-moos) smoke, 27
gallus (GHAHL-loos) rooster, 25
gemma (GHEHM-mah) jewel, 28
gladius (GLAH-dee-oos) sword, 2
habet (HAH-beht) has, 7
horologium (hoh-roh-LOH-ghee-oom) clock, 25
hortus (HOHR-toos) garden, 1
iacit (YAH-kit) throws, 14
iam (YAHM) now, 2
ianua (YA-noo-ah) door, 19
immo (EEM-moh) instead, 7
instrumentum (in-stroo-MEHN-toom) tool, 28
insula (IN-soo-lah) island, 18
iubet (YOO-beht) commands, 26
labrum (LAH-broom) lip, 17
lacrima (LAH-kree-mah) tear, 28
lectus (LEHK-toos) bed, 24
legit (LEH-ghit) reads, 4
liber (LI-bayr) book, 11
lignum (LIG-noom) wood, 16
lilium (LEE-lee-oom) lily, 24
linea (LEE-neh-ah) string, 28
lingua (LING-ghwah) tongue, 19
ludus (LOO-doos) school, 10
luna (LOO-nah) moon, 19
lupus (LOO-poos) wolf, 2

magicus (MAH-ghi-koos) magical, 27
magister (mah-GHIS-tayr) teacher, 11
malum (MAH-loom) apple, 14
margarita (mahr-ghah-REE-tah) pearl, 28
maritus (mah-REE-toos) husband, 6
medicus (MEH-di-koos) doctor, 8
mendum (MEHN-doom) mistake, 25
mensa (MEHN-sah) table, 18
minister (mi-NIS-tayr) waiter, 11
monstrat (MOHN-straht) shows, 26
monstrum (MOHN-stroom) monster, 16
mundus (MOON-doos) world, 2
murus (MOO-roos) wall, 2
nasus (NAH-soos) nose, 5
nemo (NEY-moh) nobody, 3
neque (NEH-kweh) and not, 11
nidus (NEE-doos) nest, 9
non (NOHN) not, 1
novem (NOH-vehm) nine, 28
nullus (NOOL-loos) not any, 10
numerus (NOO-meh-roos) number, 9
nummus (NOO-moos) coin, 6
nuntius (NOON-tee-oos) messenger, 8
oceanus (oh-KEE-ah-noos) ocean, 9
octo (OHK-toh) eight, 25
oculus (OH-coo-loos) eye, 1
oppidum (OHP-pi-doom) town, 12
osculum (OHS-koo-loom) kiss, 17
ostium (OH-stee-oom) door, 16
ovum (OH-voom) egg, 15
pagina (PAH-ghi-nah) page, 21
penna (PEHN-nah) feather, 22
per (PAYR) through, 19
petasus (PEH-tah-soos) hat, 3
petit (PEH-tit) goes after, 26
pila (PI-lah) ball, 21
pirum (PEE-room) pear, 14
plorat (PLOH-raht) cries, 20
poculum (POH-koo-loom) cup, 13
ponit (POH-nit) puts, 14
porcus (POHR-koos) pig, 24
porta (POHR-tah) gate, 19
post (POHST) behind, 6
pretium (PREH-tee-oom) price, 28

puella (poo-EHL-lah) girl, 18
puer (POO-ayr) boy, 1
pugnus (POOG-noos) fist, 10
pullus (POOL-loos) chick, 8
pulsat (POOL-saht) hits, 7
quattuor (KWAHT-twoor) four, 11
quia (KWEE-ah) because, 16
quid? (KWID) what? 10
quinque (KWIN-kweh) five, 11
quis? (KWIS) who? 19
quis? (KWIS) who? 6
quo? (KWOH) where to? 14
quoque (KWOH-kweh) too, 5
quot? (KWOHT) how many? 9
ramus (RAH-moos) branch, 9
regina (ray-GHEE-nah) queen, 21
regula (RAY-ghoo-lah) ruler, 25
ridet (REE-deht) laughs, 20
rivus (REE-voos) stream, 9
rosa (ROH-sah) rose, 21
sacculus (SAHK-koo-loos) purse, 6
saccus (SAHK-koos) bag, 6
sagitta (sah-GHIT-tah) arrow, 24
saxum (SAHK-soom) rock, 12
scribit (SKREE-bit) writes, 4
scutum (SKOO-toom) shield, 13
sed (SEHD) but, 3
sedet (SEH-deht) sits, 4
sella (SEHL-lah) chair, 18
septem (SEHP-tehm) seven, 25
sepulcrum (seh-POOL-khroom) grave, 27
servus (SAYR-voos) servant, 2
signum (SIG-noom) sign, 24
silva (SIL-vah) forest, 25
speculum (SPEH-koo-loom) mirror, 15
stat (STAHT) stands, 4
stella (STEHL-lah) star, 27
stilus (STI-loos) pen, 1
sub (SOOB) under, 3
sumit (SOO-mit) picks up, 14
super (SOO-payr) above, 6
taberna (tah-BAYR-nah) store, 25
tabernarius (tah-bayr-NAH-ree-oos) storekeeper, 25

tabula (TAH-boo-lah) board, 22
tectum (TEHK-toom) roof, 15
telum (TAY-loom) javelin, 13
templum (TEHM-ploom) temple, 17
tergum (TAYR-ghoom) back, 12
timet (TI-meht) fears, 20
titulus (TI-too-loos) title, 28
tres (TRAYS) three, 9
triclinium (tree-KLEE-nee-oom) dining room, 17
tyrannus (tew-RAH-noos) tyrant, 9
ubi? (OO-bee) where, 1
umerus (OO-meh-roos) shoulder, 8
unde? (OON-day) from where? 13
unus (OO-noos) one, 9
ursus (OOR-soos) bear, 6
vendit (VEHN-dit) sells, 29
ventus (VEHN-toos) wind, 5
vestigium (vehs-TI-ghee-oom) track, 16
vestimentum (vehs-ti-MEHN-toom) clothes, 17
via (VEE-ah) road, 18
videt (VEE-deht) sees, 7
villa (VIL-lah) house, 18
vinum (VEE-noom) wine, 13
vir (VEER) man, 10
vocabulum (voh-CAH-boo-loom) word, 16
vocat (VOH-kaht) calls, 26
vult (VOOLT) wants 26

English to Latin
DICTIONARY

about *de* (DAY), 18
above *super* (SOO-payr), 6
and *et* (EHT), 3
and not *neque* (NEH-kweh), 11
apple *malum* (MAH-loom), 14
arm *bracchium* (BRAHK-ki-oom), 12
arrow *sagitta* (sah-GHIT-tah), 24
at *apud* (AH-pood), 6)
back *tergum* (TAYR-ghoom), 12
bag *saccus* (SAHK-koos) 6
ball *pila* (PI-lah), 21
bathtub *balneum* (BAHL-neh-oom), 16
bear *ursus* (OOR-soos), 6
because *quia* (KWEE-ah), 16
bed *lectus* (LEHK-toos), 24
bedroom *cubiculum* (koo-BI-koo-loom), 13
behind *post* (POHST), 6
boar *aper* (AH-payr), 11
board *tabula* (TAH-boo-lah), 22
book *liber* (LI-bayr), 11
boy *puer* (POO-ayr), 1
brain *cerebrum* (keh-RAY-broom), 17
branch *ramus* (RAH-moos), 9
building *aedificium* (aye-di-FI-kee-oom), 12
but *sed* (SEHD), 3
buys *emit* (EH-mit), 29
calls *vocat* (VOH-kaht), 26
carries *fert* (FEHRT), 20
catches *capit* (KAH-pit), 14
chair *sella* (SEHL-lah), 18
chick *pullus* (POOL-loos), 8
circle *circulus* (KEER-koo-loos), 5
climbs up *ascendit* (ah-SKEHN-dit), 29
clock *horologium* (hoh-roh-LOH-ghee-oom), 25

closes *claudit* (KLOW-dit), 29
clothes *vestimentum* (vehs-ti-MEHN-toom), 17
coin *nummus* (NOO-moos), 6
commands *iubet* (YOO-beht), 26
cook *cocus* (COH-koos), 27
cooktop *focus* (FOH-koos), 8
cries *plorat* (PLOH-raht), 20
crown *corona* (koh-ROH-nah), 21
cup *poculum* (POH-koo-loom), 13
daughter *filia* (FEE-lee-ah), 19
dining room *triclinium* (tree-KLEE-nee-oom), 17
doctor *medicus* (MEH-di-koos), 8
dolphin *delphinus* (dehl-FEE-noos), 7
donkey *asinus* (AH-see-noos), 6
door *ianua* (YA-noo-ah), 19
door *ostium* (OH-stee-oom), 16
eagle *aquila* (AH-kwi-lah), 22
egg *ovum* (OH-voom), 15
eight *octo* (OHK-toh), 25
eye *oculus* (OH-coo-loos), 1
falls *cadit* (KAH-dit), 29
family *familia* (fa-MI-lee-ah), 19
farmer *colonus* (coh-LOH-noos), 10
fears *timet* (TI-meht), 20
feather *penna* (PEHN-nah), 22
field *ager* (AH-ghayr), 11
finger *digitus* (DI-ghi-toos), 1
fist *pugnus* (POOG-noos), 10
five *quinque* (KWIN-kweh), 11
flame *flamma* (FLAHM-mah), 21
food *cibus* (KI-boos), 3
forest *silva* (SIL-vah), 25
four *quattuor* (KWAHT-twoor), 11

friend *amicus* (ah-MEE-koos), 7
friend, girlfriend *amica* (ah-MEE-kah), 27
from where? *unde?* (OON-day), 13
from, away from *ab* (AHB), 2
garden *hortus* (HOHR-toos), 1
gate *porta* (POHR-tah), 19
girl *puella* (poo-EHL-lah), 18
god *deus* (DAY-oos), 8
goddess *dea* (DAY-ah), 22
goes after *petit* (PEH-tit), 26
goes down *descendit* (day-SKEHN-dit), 29
gold *aurum* (OW-room), 15
grave *sepulcrum* (seh-POOL-khroom), 27
hair *capillus* (kah-PIL-loos), 5
has *habet* (HAH-beht), 7
hat *petasus* (PEH-tah-soos), 3
hears *audit* (OW-dit), 26
hits *pulsat* (POOL-saht), 7
hole *cavus* (KAH-voos), 5
horse *equus* (EH-kwoos), 3
house *villa* (VIL-lah), 18
how many? *quot?* (KWOHT), 9
husband *maritus* (mah-REE-toos), 6
in front of *ante* (AHN-tay), 5
instead *immo* (EEM-moh), 7
is *est* (EHST), 1
is it…? *estne* (EHST-nay), 1
island *insula* (IN-soo-lah), 18
javelin *telum* (TAY-loom), 13
jewel *gemma* (GHEHM-mah), 28
kiss *osculum* (OHS-koo-loom), 17
kitchen *culina* (coo-LEE-nah), 27
knife *culter* (COOL-tayr), 11
lamb *agnus* (AHG-noos), 7
laughs *ridet* (REE-deht), 20
leaf *folium* (FOH-lee-oom), 15
letter *epistula* (eh-PIS-too-lah), 21
lily *lilium* (LEE-lee-oom), 24
lip *labrum* (LAH-broom), 17
look *ecce* (EHK-keh), 11
loves *amat* (AH-maht), 20
magical *magicus* (MAH-ghi-koos), 27
man *vir* (VEER), 10
master *dominus* (DOH-mi-noos), 2

meadow *campus* (KAHM-poos), 1
messenger *nuntius* (NOON-tee-oos), 8
mirror *speculum* (SPEH-koo-loom), 15
mistake *mendum* (MEHN-doom), 25
mistress *domina* (DOH-mi-nah), 19
monster *monstrum* (MOHN-stroom), 16
moon *luna* (LOO-nah), 19
neck *collum* (KOH-loom), 12
nest *nidus* (NEE-doos), 9
nine *novem* (NOH-vehm), 28
nobody *nemo* (NEY-moh), 3
nose *nasus* (NAH-soos), 5
not *non* (NOHN), 1
not any *nullus* (NOOL-loos), 10
now *iam* (YAHM), 2
number *numerus* (NOO-meh-roos), 9
ocean *oceanus* (oh-KEE-ah-noos), 9
one *unus* (OO-noos), 9
opens *aperit* (AH-peh-rit), 29
out of, off of *ex* (EHKS), 3
page *pagina* (PAH-ghi-nah), 21
pear *pirum* (PEE-room), 14
pearl *margarita* (mahr-ghah-REE-tah), 28
pen *stilus* (STI-loos), 1
picks up *sumit* (SOO-mit), 14
pig *porcus* (POHR-koos), 24
present *donum* (DOH-noom), 14
price *pretium* (PREH-tee-oom), 28
purse *sacculus* (SAHK-koo-loos), 6
puts *ponit* (POH-nit), 14
queen *regina* (ray-GHEE-nah), 21
reads *legit* (LEH-ghit), 4
ring *anulus* (AH-noo-loos), 3
river *fluvius* (FLOO-vee-oos), 1
road *via* (VEE-ah), 18
rock *saxum* (SAHK-soom), 12
roof *tectum* (TEHK-toom), 15
rooster *gallus* (GHAHL-loos), 25
rose *rosa* (ROH-sah), 21
ruler *regula* (RAY-ghoo-lah), 25
runs *currit* (COOR-rit), 20
says *dicit* (DEE-kit), 26
school *ludus* (LOO-doos), 10
sees *videt* (VEE-deht), 7

sells *vendit* (VEHN-dit), 29
servant *servus* (SAYR-voos), 2
seven *septem* (SEHP-tehm), 25
shield *clipeus* (KLI-peh-oos), 10
shield *scutum* (SKOO-toom), 13
shoe *calceus* (KAHL-keh-oos), 3
shoulder *umerus* (OO-meh-roos), 8
shows *monstrat* (MOHN-straht), 26
sign *signum* (SIG-noom), 24
silver *argentum* (ahr-GHEN-toom), 15
sits *sedet* (SEH-deht), 4
sky *caelum* (KAYE-loom), 13
sleeps *dormit* (DOHR-mit), 4
smoke *fumus* (FOO-moos), 27
son *filius* (FEE-lee-oos), 5
spider *aranea* (ah-RAH-neh-ah), 24
spirit *anima* (AH-ni-mah), 27
stands *stat* (STAHT), 4
star *astrum* (AHS-troom), 13
star *stella* (STEHL-lah), 27
stick *baculum* (BAH-koo-loom), 12
store *taberna* (tah-BAYR-nah), 25
storekeeper *tabernarius* (tah-bayr-NAH-ree-oos), 25
stream *rivus* (REE-voos), 9
string *linea* (LEE-neh-ah), 28
student *discipulus* (di-SKI-poo-loos), 10
sword *gladius* (GLAH-dee-oos), 2
table *mensa* (MEHN-sah), 18
tail *cauda* (KOW-dah), 22
teacher *magister* (mah-GHIS-tayr), 11
tear *lacrima* (LAH-kree-mah), 28
temple *templum* (TEHM-ploom), 17
ten *decem* (DEH-kehm), 28
the end *finis* (FEE-nis), 1
thinks *cogitat* (COH-ghee-taht), 4
three *tres* (TRAYS), 9
through *per* (PAYR), 19
throws *iacit* (YAH-kit), 14
title *titulus* (TI-too-loos), 28
to *ad* (AHD), 5
tongue *lingua* (LING-ghwah), 19
too *quoque* (KWOH-kweh), 5
tool *instrumentum* (in-stroo-MEHN-toom), 28

town *oppidum* (OHP-pi-doom), 12
track *vestigium* (vehs-TI-ghee-oom), 16
two *duo* (DOO-oh), 9
tyrant *tyrannus* (tew-RAH-noos), 9
under *sub* (SOOB), 3
waiter *minister* (mi-NIS-tayr), 11
walks *ambulat* (AHM-boo-laht), 2
wall *murus* (MOO-roos), 2
war *bellum* (BEHL-loom), 15
water *aqua* (AH-kwah), 22
what? *quid?* (KWID), 10
where *ubi?* (OO-bee), 1
where to? *quo?* (KWOH), 14
while *dum* (DOOM), 4
who? *quis?* (KWIS), 19
who? *quis?* (KWIS), 6
why? *cur?* (COOR), 16
wind *ventus* (VEHN-toos), 5
window *fenestra* (feh-NEHS-trah), 22
wine *vinum* (VEE-noom), 13
wing *ala* (AH-lah), 24
with, together with *cum* (KOOM), 2
wolf *lupus* (LOO-poos), 2
woman *femina* (FAY-mi-nah), 18
wood *lignum* (LIG-noom), 16
word *vocabulum* (voh-CAH-boo-loom), 16
world *mundus* (MOON-doos), 2
writes *scribit* (SKREE-bit), 4

Classroom Lessons, Discussions, and Activities

Instructions:

The 30 lessons of *Picta Dicta Latin Primer* (vol. 1) focus on the grammar and vocabulary necessary to get students reading Latin stories. The activities in *Classroom Lessons, Discussions, and Activities* are optional exercises designed to bring Latin into the the classroom. These activities complement the exercises in the Latin Primer app and workbook, but focus on different grammar and vocabulary--the grammar and vocabulary necessary for simple Latin conversation.

The *Classroom Lessons, Discussions, and Activities* should be introduced in order; however they are not keyed to the 30 lessons of the Picta Dicta Latin Primer at all. This gives a teacher the flexibility not to proceed to the next lesson until the students are very comfortable with the all the previous lessons. Once the class gets to some of the more challenging exercises, there is enough material to work on for several weeks. We recommend that teachers use these exercises whenever there is extra time to fill, or on a designated day of the week.

The discussions are designed around questions. We encourage teachers to ask these discussion questions of the class and give the students an opportunity to see if they know the answer. If they do not, we include answers to all the questions for the teacher to supply them.

When students learn additional words in these exercises, it is a good idea to have them write them down in the Student Workbooks in the *Vocabula* section. Even though these words will not appear on the quizzes or lesson exercises, it is helpful for the students to have them all in one place.

If a teacher does not wish to do these classroom activities or does not get very far in the year, this will not cause any trouble for the students using the *Picta Dicta Latin Primer*.

CAP I: Latin and the Romans

LESSON / DISCUSSION

What is Latin?

Latin was the language spoken by the ancient Romans.

Who were the Romans?

The Romans were the ancient people who originally came from the Italian city of Rome.

1. Can anyone show me where Italy is on the map?
2. Can anyone show me where Rome is on the map?
3. When did the Romans live?

Why are the Romans important today?

The Romans were a very warlike people and defeated the cities and people who lived around them. Eventually they conquered almost all of Europe and some parts of Africa and Asia as well. Their empire lasted for many hundreds of years and changed the world a lot. Many of the things that we still do today began with the Romans.

Why is Latin important?

For lots of reasons! But here are three big ones:

- Learning Latin helps us learn so much about the way ancient people thought about everything. This helps us read and understand our history.
- Many of the best books ever written were written in Latin. Learning Latin allows us to read them.
- Latin is also the foundation for much of the English language. Many English words and English grammar concepts come from Latin. By learning Latin, we learn to read, write, and understand English better.

Is Latin still used today?

Most ancient Romans were a lot like people today: they did not always speak Latin the way they were supposed to. They made up new ways of saying things and mixed their language with other languages until eventually they were not speaking Latin any more—they were speaking Spanish, Italian, French, and Romanian.

But in schools, monasteries and colleges, people have learned Latin since Roman times. Over the last thousand years, most of the best authors, best pastors, best thinkers, and best lawmakers have studied Latin in school. Now it's your turn.

CAP II: Around the Classroom

ACTIVITY

Salvete / Salve

A teacher should greet the students by saying "Salvete!" ("Greetings!"). The students should reply ("Salve"). When the students ask why the two greetings are different, the teacher should explain that *salvete* is said to many people, and *salve* is said to just one person.

LESSON / DISCUSSION

Did Romans have words for things like we have today?

Not exactly. Many things we have today like computers, televisions, telephones, cars, planes did not exist when the Romans spoke Latin.

However, most things in our time are a lot like the old things in Roman times, and we can use old Latin words for new things. The Romans did not have electric lights, but they did have oil lamps and candles. So we use the word for oil lamp (*lucerna*) for an electric light. The Romans did not have little whiteboards, but they did have wax tablets that the students would write on in school. So we use the word for tablet (*tabella*) for a personal white board.

Sometimes, we have words for new things that aren't like anything the Romans had, like refrigerators. Even so, Latin words are made up of little parts that can explain a new thing very well. If an ancient Roman came across the word *refrigeratorium*, he wouldn't know exactly what it meant—but he would know you meant "a place where things are kept at a cool temperature": *orium* usually means a place where something is done, *frigerat* means "to make cold", *re* can mean to do something "repeatedly". In fact, Latin is so good at piecing together new meanings that new English words (like refrigerator) are often just made up from Latin parts.

ACTIVITY

Ecce / Quid est?

In this activity the teacher points to things (with a finger, laser pointer, or pointing rod) around the room and calls out their Latin names, like this: "*Ecce tabula*" ("Behold the board!")

The teacher explains that "ecce" is a word you use when pointing something out. It would be like saying "Behold!" or "Look!" or "Lo!" or "Here is a …"

Once a teacher has called out the name of something, the students are made to repeat it in unison. The teacher should ensure that the proper pronunciation is imitated. A teacher may also choose to single out a student or a group of students to repeat at this point.

After students have gotten good at repeating, the teacher should switch to a question: *quid est?* ("What is it?") The teacher should ask *Quid est?* of all the things in the classroom with the students responding in Latin.

Finally, a teacher may ask the students to pair up (still in their seats) and do the exercise on their own, taking turns as they ask and answer. The teacher walks around the room and listens to make sure everyone is doing the exercise properly.

At some point the teacher should have the students copy down the words from the board into the *Vocabula* section of the Student Workbook (on pg. 63) for their own reference. By writing the words out on their own, they practice the spelling.

The teacher should introduce vocabulary in this chapter in several sections and at least over a couple of weeks, cycling between introduction, group questions, questions in pairs, discussion of the meaning, copying down and completing the worksheets at the end of the chapter.

Quae sunt?

Once students are very familiar with the *quid est?*, the teacher can teach them *quae sunt?* ("What are they?"). Pointing to two things, the teacher asks "Quae sunt?" and the student respond using *et* ("and") between their answers. For example: "Quae sunt?" "tabula *et* lucerna".

Since the students have not yet learned the plural endings for all these kinds of words, it is important not to ask *quae sunt?* of two of the same kind of thing *yet*!

VOCABULARY

A:
tabula — a board (white/chalk board)
solum — floor
lucerna — a lamp (any light fixture)
sella — a chair
mensa — a large tabletop (teacher's desk)
mensula — a small tabletop (student's desk)
fenestra — window
tectum — ceiling
ianua — door

B:
loculus — compartment for storing things (space under a desk or drawer)
liber — a scroll (book)
charta — paper
tabella — little wax tablet (personal white board)
calamus — ink pen (or marker)
plumbum — lead lump (pencil)
capsa — book carrying case (book bag)
lagoena — a largish bottle (water bottle)
libellus — *a notebook* (this can be used for the Student Workbook)

C:
pluteus — shelf

pictura — painting (or photograph)
scirpiculus — a basket made of rushes sometimes used to throw garbage into (trashcan)
proiectorium* — a projector (tool which throws forward)
ansa — door knob
computatrum* — computer (tool which calculates)

D:
poculum — a cup or mug
tegumentum — cover (binder)
cafea* — coffee
lectrinum — a lectern
flabellum — a hand fan (an electric fan)
tabula geographica — map
magister — male teacher
magistra — female teacher
discipulus — male student
discipula — female student

CAP III: Abecetum

LESSON / DISCUSSION

Where does our alphabet come from?

The English alphabet actually comes from the Latin alphabet. Almost all of the letters we know were Latin letters as well. But in Roman times, every letter made one sound instead of several, so phonics was a lot easier.

Are there any English letters that you have not seen in any Latin words?

The Romans did not have a 'w' or a 'j'. The Romans did not make those sounds in their words, so they did not have letters to make them. Sort of like in English we do not have a letter for the ps sound or the y sound (listen to audio recording).

ACTIVITY

Latin Phonics

Write all the letters of the alphabet on the board or have a poster where students can see it clearly. Use a pointer to point to different letters and have the entire class shout out the proper Latin sound. Start with a few letters and work your way back and forth until you get through the whole alphabet. When you come to a "w" or "j", the students should be completely silent. That way, when someone blurts out the English sound, everybody hears and the mistake is obvious—and a little funny.

> a, b, c, d, e, f, g, h, i, k, l, m, n, o, p, qu, r, s, t, u, v, x, y, z

The letters that will be tricky are:

- r which is soft and trilled
- v which is sounds half way between a v and a w with the lips touching but buzzing.
- y which sounds half way between i and oo

CHANT

Abecetum

These are the Roman letter names according to the Romans. It is fun to teach them this chant and then have them race to see who can do it the fastest.

> a, b, c, d, e, f, g, h, i, k, l, m, n, o, p, qu, r, s, t, u, x, y, z

You may notice that there is no letter name for v in the abecetum. This is because the Romans treated 'u' and 'v' as the same letter.

LESSON

A diphthong is two vowels that make one sound together. In Latin there are six diphthongs:

>ae, au, eu, oe, ui, ei

Just like in the exercise with the Latin letters, write the dipthongs on the board. Point to them and make the students shout out the proper sound.

As a challenge, you can add some vowel combinations that are *not* diphthongs if you wish: ii, uu, iu. These non-diphthongs are pronounced as two syllables. You could have them shout "not a diphthong" and then pronounce it as two syllables.

CAP IV: Numeri Faciles
("Easy Numbers")

LESSON/DISCUSSION

What are numerals?

Write a math problem or two on the board at a level that the students can do, but write the names of the numbers and symbols out instead of using numerals: e.g., eight times eight equals what? or eight thousand four hundred and thirty seven times twenty four would be what? Have them solve it on their white boards. Afterwards, see how many of them convert the problem into numerals first. Ask them why they did not just solve the problem with the number names. They will probably answer that it is more confusing with long names. *That* is what a numeral is for.

Where do our numerals come from?

Our English numerals do not come from Latin or Greek, but from Indian mathematicians who came up with special symbols for 0 - 9. Arabic mathematicians picked them up from the Indians, and later European mathematicians picked them up from the Arabs.

How did the Romans write numbers?

The Romans used numerals as well, but they used certain letters to mean certain numbers and then added them together to make bigger numbers.

See if any (or all) of the students already know any or all of the Roman numerals from I – X:

> I, II, III, IV, V, VI, VII, VIII, VIII, IX, X

Make large flashcards (or just 8.5 x 11 sheets) with the Roman numerals on them. Mix them up and hold them up. Students should shout out the English number for each numeral.

Once they are all shouting out the numbers well, switch to whiteboards. Have the students write out the English numbers or English numerals for the Roman numeral held up.

Once they've mastered that, call out an English number and have students write the Roman numeral on their boards.

ROMAN NUMBERS

Hold up fingers or paper flashcards with Roman numerals to teach students the Roman numbers from I – X. If things are going well, you can go to XX as well.

VOCABULARY

> A:
> *unus* — one
> *duo* — two
> *tres* — three

quattuor — four
quinque — five
sex — six
septem — seven
octo — eight
novem — nine
decem — ten

B:
undecim — eleven
duodecim — twelve
tredecim — thirteen
quattuordecim — fourteen
quindecim — fifteen
sedecim — sixteen
septendecim — seventeen
duodeviginti — eighteen
undeviginti — nineteen
viginti — twenty

ACTIVITY

Quot sunt? (How many are there?)

The question *quot?* in Latin means "how many"? Ask *quot sunt?* while holding up fingers or of things you are pointing out around the room. Then advance to simple math problems in Latin and have them write the proper answers on their whiteboards, either as Roman numerals or whole Latin words. Make it a speed contest. Whenever a student gets correct in 5 seconds, have them give themselves a tally mark on the corner of their whiteboard. Give out a prize for the winner.

> Quot sunt unus et unus? Duo. ("How many are one and one?")
> Quot sunt unus et duo? Tres. ("How many are one and two?")

Unus, duo, tres

See how fast the students can count from *unus* to *decem* or *unus* to *viginti*. Have them do it backwards. Give out prizes for the fastest.

CAP V: Personal Pronouns

LESSON / DISCUSSION

Has anyone ever heard of the phrase "first person"? What does it mean?

Everybody put your hand on your chest. This is the first person. It's different for everybody. For me, the first person is [point to self dramatically] me! But for [name of a random student], the first person is who [let the student say "me"]. The first person is always "me" no matter who says it. Now if we are going to use English properly, we should say "I". Everybody put your hand on your chest and puff it out some and say "I". "I" is the first person—or maybe we should say "I" *am* the first person.

So if "I" is the first person, who is the "second person"? What does that mean?

> [Point to a random student, look right at him, point at him, and say his name.] Billy, you are the 2nd person. Anyone know why Billy was the 2nd person? He was the second person because I was talking *to* him. Is the second person now? Nope, not anymore. I'm talking to Sally right now, so she is the second person. Everyone point at me and look at me. Who is the second person? "You" is the second person. Now everybody put your hand on your own chest and say "I"—that's the first person. Now everybody point to me and say "you"—that's the second person.

So if "I" is the first person and "you" is the second person, who is the "third person"? What does that mean?

> [Point to another random student, do not look at her, and say her name.] Gretchen is the third person! Why is Gretchen the third person? She is the third person because I am not talking *to* her but *about* her. Everybody point to the person on your right, but keep looking at me! That is the third person. He, she, or it! Wait? Can "it" be a person? In grammar, even "it" can be a person, but only the third person. Who is the third person? "He, she, it" is the third person. But be careful not to look at them, because that would turn them into the second person.

ACTIVITY

Persons Game (English)

Have the students mirror your movements as you call out the persons: first second, and third. Start by putting your hand on your chest, exclaim "First", and have them do likewise. Point to one student in the front row and say "Second". The students should all be pointing at you and should also exclaim, "Second!". Finally, point over to the side while still looking at the student in the front row and exclaim, "Third!". Students should again imitate.

Now, have them mirror your motions while calling out the persons as you change between different persons at random. Switch them up. Go fast, then slow. For third person, try pointing in random directions (just not toward the students). Once they get good at it, stop shouting out the person yourself and let them do it. If someone says the wrong thing, it'll stick out. Have a good laugh about it.

Once they have gotten good at calling out "first", "second", "third", start calling out, "I", "You", "He". Explain that really it is "He, she, it" but that takes too long to say and it works better in Latin to use "he".

After this becomes easy, introduce the plural versions of the persons: "we, you all, and they". The hand signal for "we" is to gesture in a circle once; the hand signal for "you all" is to use both hands and gesture out toward the audience; the hand signal for "they" is to point to one side with both hands.

You should start having the students chant "first person, plural", "second person, plural", and "third person, plural". Once that becomes easy, switch to "we", "you all" (or "ya'll"), and "they".

Once the students are very good at getting all the English pronouns in English switching up the answers, it is time to move onto the Latin equivalents.

Persons Game (Latin)

Begin with the Latin equivalents for "I", "You", and "he": *ego, tu, is*. Move the through the hand signals and switch them up, always having the student mirror your motions. The lazy ones will stop using their hands, and you have to make them.

Then move on to the Latin equivalents for the plural pronouns "we", "you all", and "they": *nos, vos, ii*. Again, mix them up until the student are familiar with all of them.

CAP VI: *Sum*

LESSON / DISCUSSION

Does anyone know different persons for the English verb "is"?

Write the sentence *I _____ a student.* on the board. Have a random student put his hand on his chest, and ask him to complete the sentence. Hopefully, the student will say, "I *am* a student." If the student doesn't, prompt him by asking "Who *are* you?". When the student says, "I *am* a student." Ask the class what *person* the English verb "am" is in, and what *number*. If nobody gets it, place your hand on your chest and exaggerate, "I *am* a student." Someone should respond that "am" is in the first person, singular.

Repeat the exercise for the 2nd-person, singular. Have a student point to another student, look at that student, and fill in the blank for *You _____ a student*. This time have the class identify it as the 2nd-person, singular.

Finally, do the same thing for 3rd-person, singular. Have a student point to another student and look at you while filling in the blank for *He _____ a student*. This time have the class identify it as 3rd-person, singular.

The verb "is" is the only verb in modern English that has very different forms for different persons.

Now play the persons game just a bit, as you do 1st-, 2nd-, and 3rd-person, singular for the following: *I am a student, you are a student, he is a student*. You can also for fun have the students switch it to "You are *not* a student." whenever they point at you.

After this makes sense, show the students how in the plural the form is always just "are": *we are, you all are, they are*. If you like, you can play the persons game a bit more to make your point.

Sum

In Latin, the verb that means "is" also has special forms for the different persons.

Go through the same steps as in the last lesson to teach students the different forms for the verb *sum* one by one:

Ego sum. ("I am.")
Tu es. ("You are.")
Is est. ("He is.")
Nos sumus. ("We are.")
Vos estis. ("You all are.")
Ii sunt. ("They are.")

Once they have mastered the forms, you can add a noun to make it mean something. This is easy, but you will have to change the noun form to plural for *nos, vos,* and *ii*. You should *not* attempt to explain how plural works for everything at this point, but just pick something that works:

Sg.
Homo ("a person")
Discipulus ("a male student")
Discipula ("a female student")

Pl.
Homines ("people")
Discipuli ("students")
Discipulae ("female students")

Ego homo sum. ("I am a person.")
Tu homo es. ("You are a person.")
Is homo est. ("He is a person.")
Nos homines sumus. ("We are people.")
Vos homines estis. ("You all are people.")
Ii homines sunt. ("They are people.")

CAP VII: *Surgo*

LESSON / DISCUSSION

Does anyone know the difference between "knowest" and "knoweth"?

In older English, like in the King James edition of the Bible, even normal verbs like know and run change their endings according to person. Four hundred years ago, it would have been correct to write "I know", "Thou knowest", and "He knoweth".

Draw a chart on the board with 1st, 2nd, and 3rd persons, singular and plural. Fill out the chart as follows:

	Sg.	Pl.
1st	I know	We know
2nd	Thou know-est	Ye know*
3rd	He know-eth	They know

*In some forms of older English, "you" was used instead of "ye", but this isn't important for the students here. Kids, of course, prefer learning the more unusual form "ye" to "you".

The dashes are added here just to separate the verb stem from the ending—they are not necessary. Use the hand signals to have kids practice using antiquated English persons for English several verbs. Let the students pick some English verbs to do this with. Once students are comfortable with these forms, consider assigning them to try using these forms at home at the dinner table to see what their parents think.

SURGERE

In Latin, all verbs work like in older English—their endings change with the person. For example, the Latin verb *surg-it* means "He stands up." But *surg-o* means "I stand up." The verb *surg-is* means "You stand up." Draw a chart on the board as follows:

	Sg.	Pl.
1st	ego surg-o	nos surg-imus
2nd	tu surg-is	vos surg-itis
3rd	is surg-it	ii surg-unt

The dashes are again added here just to separate the verb stem from the ending. These same endings will be used for almost all verbs in Latin to show person. Use the hand signals to work through all three persons, singular and plural.

In Latin, the personal pronouns *ego, tu, is, nos, vos, ii* are not actually necessary. You can leave them out because the endings tell you the person on their own. Go through the same exercise again but without the personal pronouns.

	Sg.	**Pl.**
1ˢᵗ	surg-o	surg-imus
2ⁿᵈ	surg-is	surg-itis
3ʳᵈ	surg-it	surg-unt

After students master *surgo*, you should switch to different verbs and do the hand signals exercise until it is very natural. Here are some verbs to practice with:

- *consid-o* — "I sit down"
- *animadvert-o* — "I notice"
- *leg-o* — "I read"
- *gem-o* — "I groan"
- *curr-o* — "I run"
- *bib-o* — "I drink"

CAP VIII: Commands

ACTIVITY

In this lesson, you will demonstrate the difference between *commands* and *statements of fact* in English. You will be using a teaching method where students *act out* the commands that you give them. This would be chaotic (and disastrous!) if they were to actually act out many of these commands with their whole bodies. So, instead, you will need to develop a nice and tidy sign language of sorts for the different actions. It is up to the teacher what sign language to assign, but it is absolutely essential that it be *orderly, clear, and confined to the desk.*

Explain to the class that you are going to give them some orders in English and that they are to obey the orders immediately. But instead of actually doing the actions, they are going to do a sort of sign language.

Start with the word, *rise*. Say *rise* to the students, and make sure that they all rise to their feet in an orderly fashion. If they do not do it right, it helps to have them do it a few times until they do it well.

Then proceed to the word, *sit*. Say *sit* to the students, and make sure that they all sit in unison in an orderly fashion again. Have them rise and sit a couple times, giving the commands.

Now explain to the students that as they rise they must say, "I rise", in unison. And when they sit, they must say, "I sit" as they do it. Again, have them do this a couple times.

The next verb to use is *run*. Obviously, if they actually ran, chaos would ensue. So, instead, explain to the students that they must make two fingers "run" across the table, instead of actually running. Once they understand that, command them in English. *Run*! Make sure that they run with their fingers and they do it in a very orderly, standardized way. They should say, "I run" as they do this.

The next verb to use is *stop*. Teach them that they should make their fingers "freeze" instantly and say, "I stop". You can have some fun with rise, and sit, run, and stop.

Add *drink* in the same way. Let them pretend that they have a cup and are taking a sip *in an orderly way*.

Add *read*. Let them pretend that they have a book and flip a page.

Add *notice*. Let them look to one side and pretend to see something and say, "oh".

Add *groan*. Have them make a moderate groan as if they are disappointed.

The key with all of this is to keep it very regimented and orderly. Otherwise, elementary kids can get too carried away. This is a great time to be very, very strict about their motions.

What is the difference between a "command" and a "statement of fact"?

A command is telling someone to do or not to do something. A command is neither true or false. So if I give a command like, "Stop!", it makes no sense to say, "That's true!" or "That's not true." Instead, you say, "Yes, I will!" or "No, I won't!"

A statement of fact is saying that something is true or not true. A statement of fact is either true or false. So, if I make a statement of fact like, "All dogs are blue!", it makes sense to say, "That's true" or "That's really false!". Saying, "Yes, I will" or "No, I won't!" doesn't make sense with statements of fact usually.

A verb giving a command in grammar is called *imperative*, and a verb making a statement of fact is called *indicative*.

ACTIVITY

Call out sentences in English that are either commands or statements of fact. If a sentence is a command, the students should shout out, "Imperative!" If it is a statement of fact, the students should shout out, "Indicative!"

Here are some sample sentences, or the teacher can make up his or her own:

"Sit, dog!"	*imperative*
"The dog sits!"	*indicative*
"I am happy!"	*indicative*
"Be happy!"	*imperative*
"Fall down a manhole!"	*imperative*
"You fell down a manhole."	*indicative*

LATIN IMPERATIVE

In Latin, an imperative for a verb like *surgo* is formed by adding the letter -e to the end of the stem: *surge*. This forms the singular imperative, so this only works when commanding *one* person. Once you have taught the students this ending and what it means, command *one* student, "*Surge!*" When that student rises to his feet, make him say, "*Surgo*" just like the students did in English earlier. Then command several student (individually) using "surge" to rise.

After you are finished, use "*Conside*" one by one to make them all sit down. Always, make them use the indicative (*surgo, considio,* etc.) to say what they are doing. Add the other verbs in the same way: *bibe, lege, animadverte, curre, consiste*.

The plural imperative for a verb like *surgo* is formed by adding the ending -ite to the end of the stem: *surgite*. Once you have taught this to the students, command them all at once using *surgite, considite, currite, consistite, bibite, animadvertite, legite*. As always, the students should say the indicative as they complete the action.

ACTIVITY

Now that the students know the basic imperative and indicative forms, you have all the tools you need to work them on all kinds of verbs. You command them either individually (e.g., *surge*) or as a group (e.g., *surgite*). Then occasionally, switch gears and have them use the hand signals to conjugate the verb in all three persons. This is a great tool to help them build verb vocabulary while practicing the forms.

Here is a list of basic verbs that follow the same pattern and can be taught this way.

surg-o	to rise
consid-o	to sit down
curr-o	to run
consist-o	to stop in place
bib-o	to drink
leg-o	to read
animadvert-o	to notice
gem-o	to groan
cad-o	to fall
quaer-o	to search for
pell-o	to shove
toll-o	to lift
can-o	to sing
claud-o	to close
carp-o	to pluck
comed-o	to eat
flu-o	to flow (like water)
fund-o	to pour out
iung-o	to join
merg-o	to dip (under water)
ping-o	to paint
rad-o	to shave
solv-o	to untie (a knot)

These can be introduced slowly over a couple of weeks as students get used to the forms.

CAP IX: Prohibitions

LESSON / DISCUSSION

What does the word "prohibition" mean?

A prohibition is a command *not* to do something.

How does someone make a prohibition in English?

Ask for examples of prohibitions in English from the classroom. Try to get students to use different forms of prohibitions in English. For example, "Don't eat my cereal!"

"Do not eat my cereal!"
"Thou shalt not eat of my cereal!"

Have all the students a few minutes some time making up their own prohibitions for the class.

NEGATIVE LATIN IMPERATIVE

One way in Latin to make a prohibition is to use a negative imperative—a command *not* to do something. A Latin imperative is made negative by using the word *ne* first. For example,

Ne surge!	("Don't rise, you!")
Ne considite!	("Don't sit down, ya'll!")
Ne bibe!	("Don't drink, you!")
Ne pingite!	("Don't paint, ya'll!")

ACTIVITY

Now that the students know how to do both positive and negative commands, do the imperative exercise where you give students commands in Latin again. However, this time you should occasionally throw in *ne*. Whenever *ne* is added first, the students should *not* follow the sign language for the command. Thus, the exercise becomes a kind of reverse of the game "Simeon says". A teacher could even choose to have people be "out" whenever they do an action that was prohibited or don't do an action that was commanded.

145

CAP X: *Non* and Negative Statements

LESSON / DISCUSSION

How does someone make a negative statement in English?

In English, we add the word "not" to make a statement negative. We usually add the word "does" or "do" as well. Have everybody in the class make up a negative statement.

NEGATIVE LATIN STATEMENT (INDICATIVE)

In Latin, to make an indicative verb negative, the word *non* is added first. For example,

Non surgo.	("I do not rise.")
Non cadunt.	("They do not fall.")
Non claudimus.	("We do not close.")

There is nothing like "do" or "does" in Latin, so that is all you have to do. The word *non* should be in front of the verb. Have the students practice doing the hand persons drill with a negative verb:

non surgo	*non surgimus*
non surgis	*non surgitis*
non surgis	*non surgunt*

Practice switching between imperatives and indicatives, negative and positive. Give some commands, positive and negative. Then switch to the persons drill, positive and negative. Use extra persons worksheets to practice writing the proper persons for various verbs students have learned.

CAP XI: E-Stem Verbs

LESSON / DISCUSSION

What would happen if we had a verb like time-o (or time-t)? What would the endings be like for the persons?

Try to get a student or two to attempt to add the regular verb endings *o, is, it, imus, itis, unt* to the verb stem. The result *should* be a minor disaster because it is *really* hard to say, especially fast:

timeo	*timeimus*
timeis	*timeitis*
timeit	*timeunt*

Have fun trying to get students to say this fast until the whole class comes to the conclusion that it just does *not* work well.

Why is it so hard to add the verb endings to the verb time-o (or time-t)?

It is hard to pronounce two vowels next to each other if you pronounce them separately, like you do in Latin. To illustrate this point, write these made-up words on the board and have the students try to pronounce them, making sure to pronounce each vowel separately:

e-u-i-o
a-i-o-u
e-e-i-i-o-o-u-u

If we drop some consonants between each vowel, it is *much, much* easier:

pe-nu-pi-no
a-mi-to-du
te-ne-pi-ni-bo-bo-lu-lu

To drive the point home, it may be necessary to have students try to say the vowels only 5x fast versus the version with consonants in between.

VARIABLE VOWELS

The Romans agreed--it is too hard to pronounce a bunch of vowels together separately. What they actually would have said was this:

tímeo	*timémus*
tímes	*timétis*
tímet	*tíment*

They *hated* putting a bunch of vowels in a row, especially if they were difficult to say. Instead, the endings they use for verbs have *drop-out* vowels--vowels that drop out if there is already

147

another vowel. Here the drop-out vowels are marked in parentheses:

o	(i)mus
(i)s	(i)tis
(i)t	(u)nt

INDICATIVE E-STEM VERBS

When the drop-out vowels drop out after the -e in the stem, the forms are as follows:

tíme-o	timé-mus
tíme-s	timé-tis
tíme-t	tíme-nt

Notice that the -o is *not* a drop-out vowel. It stays, and is not very difficult to say after the letter -e.

IMPERATIVE E-STEM VERBS

The imperative endings *also* have drop-out vowels:

Sg.	Pl.
(e)	(i)te

Otherwise, the Romans would have had to say *timee* and *timeite*! Instead the imperative forms are as follows:

Sg.	Pl.
tíme	timéte

ACTIVITY

Now that the students know the basic imperative and indicative forms of e-stem verbs like *time-o*, students should practice doing imperative and indicative e-stem verbs while reviewing the regular consonant-stem verbs:

Command them either individually (e.g., *surge*) or as a group (e.g., *surgite*), and have them do sign-language obedience (like before). Then occasionally, switch gears and have them use the hand signals to conjugate the verb in all three persons. This is a great tool to help them build verb vocabulary while practicing the forms.

The following are e-stem verbs that can be fun to practice in the classroom:

tace-o	to be silent
mane-o	to wait
ride-o	to laugh
responde-o	to answer
vide-o	to see
habe-o	to have

pare-o	to obey
time-o	to be afraid
vale-o	to be strong
tene-o	to hold in one's grip
terge-o	to wipe
iace-o	to be lying down
aude-o	to be bold
move-o	to move (something—not yourself)

These should be introduced slowly over a couple of weeks as students get used to the forms, and it is important to mix in review words as they learn the new ones. It is also a good idea to throw some quizzes in where students have to remember which verbs are e-stem and which are consonant-stem. Use speed drills with persons worksheets to practice e-stem verbs as well.

CAP XII: A-Stem Verbs

LESSON / DISCUSSION

What would happen if we had a verb with a stem like ama-? What would the endings be like for the persons?

If the students remember the principle of the drop-out vowels, they may be able to come to the conclusion that the verb would be like this:

ama-o	*ama-mus*
ama-s	*ama-tis*
ama-t	*ama-nt*

This is...again...*almost* correct! The problem this time is with the 1st-person singular form, *ama-o*. As we learned before, -o is *not* a drop-out vowel. But it sounds *terrible* to say, *ama-o*. Have students try saying this a bit to drive the point home. The vowels *a* and *o* are just too close to each other to sound right when pronounced one after the other.

To solve it, Latin does something very, very rare--the *a* in the stem drops out to become *am-o*. This is not something that normally happens. Usually, a stem of a verb will *always* remain unaltered. But this is an exception.

Unfortunately, dropping the -a in the first form makes it difficult to recognize a-stem verbs from the 1st-person form. Most courses would write *am-o* but this disguises the fact that it has an a-stem. In this course, we will write it *ama-o,* with a slash through the *a* to prevent misunderstanding.

INDICATIVE I-STEM VERBS

When the drop-out vowels drop out after the -a in the stem and the *a-o* exception is remembered, the forms are as follows:

ám-o	*amá-mus*
áma-s	*amá-tis*
áma-t	*áma-nt*

IMPERATIVE A-STEM VERBS

When the imperative endings are applied with the drop-out vowels to A-stem verbs, the forms are as follows:

Sg.	**Pl.**
áma	*amáte*

ACTIVITY

Now that the students know the basic imperative and indicative forms of A-stem verbs like *ama-o*, students should practice doing imperative and indicative a-stem verbs while reviewing the regular consonant-stem, e-stem, and i-stem verbs:

Command them either individually (e.g., *surge*) or as a group (e.g., *surgite*), and have them do sign-language obedience (like before). Then occasionally, switch gears and have them use the hand signals to conjugate the verb in all three persons. This is a great tool to help them build verb vocabulary while practicing the forms.

The following are i-stem verbs that can be fun to practice in the classroom:

ama-o	to love
pulsa-o	to punch
roga-o	to ask
plora-o	to cry (audibly)
numera-o	to count
habita-o	to dwell
intra-o	to enter
porta-o	to transport
ambula-o	to walk
monstra-o	to point with the finger
latra-o	to bark (like a dog)
bala-o	to bleet (like a sheep)
ulula-o	to howl (like a wolf)
erra-o	to wander about
nata-o	to swim
vola-o	to fly

These should again be introduced slowly over a couple of weeks, and it is important to mix in review words as they learn the new ones. Use quizzes, persons worksheets to reinforce.